SPIRITUAL QUEST

In Verse

A Literary Criticism
Of Ricaredo Demetillo's
Religious Poetry

GILBERT LUIS R. CENTINA III

Spiritual Quest in Verse: A Literary Criticism of Ricaredo Demetillo's Religious Poetry. Copyright © 2021 by Centiramo Publishing. All rights reserved. No part of this book may be reproduced in any form or by any electronic or mechanical means, including information storage and retrieval systems, without written permission from the copyright owner except in the case of a reviewer, who may quote brief passages embodied in critical articles in a review.

Published in the United States by Centiramo Publishing, New York, NY
Visit us on the web at *www.centiramopublishing.com* and *www.gilbertluisrcentinaiii.com*
For inquiries, email *info@centiramopublishing.com*

Second Edition
Art consultant: *Janet Frances White*
Interior design and book layout: *Pierce Centina*
Charcoal sketch of Ricaredo Demetillo © 2017 by *Vicente Jáuregui*
The photo of Ricaredo Demetillo on page xviii is from the Demetillo family photo archives through the *Philippines Graphic* magazine online.

Library of Congress Cataloging-in-Publication Data

Names: Centina, Gilbert Luis R., III, 1947-2020, author.
Title: Spiritual quest in verse : a literary criticism of Ricaredo
   Demetillo's religious poetry / Gilbert Luis R. Centina III.
Description: Second edition. | New York, NY : Centiramo Publishing, [2021]
   | Includes bibliographical references. | Summary: "This book delves into
   the religious character, substance and symbolisms in Ricaredo
   Demetillo's poetry rather than into its form or structure. As a
   religious poet, Demetillo--one of the Philippines' most gifted
   poets--undertakes a spiritual journey, which is actually a flight from
   wrong values, hypocritical religion, crumbling civilization, and moral
   corruption. For Demetillo, God is the God of the living, not of the
   dead. Heaven and hell are within man himself; through self-knowledge,
   man regains his lost paradise. Love alone heals and forgives After his
   spiritual journey, Demetillo finds the immanent God through his kinship
   with fellow artists. Art is calvary; the artist participates in Christ's
   calvary. Restless in spirit, the artist can rest in God because he alone
   is able to fill the void within the artist's heart. The artist is God's
   instrument in this world to proclaim and glorify him. Through the life
   and art of the artist, God is completed in the world of the tangibles"--
   Provided by publisher.
Identifiers: LCCN 2021011200 | ISBN 9781734725681 (paperback)
Subjects: LCSH: Demetillo, Ricaredo--Criticism and interpretation. |
   Demetillo, Ricaredo--Religion.
Classification: LCC PR9550.9.D4 Z25 2021 | DDC 821/.914--dc23
LC record available at https://lccn.loc.gov/2021011200

Manufactured in the United States of America
6 8 10 12 14 16 18 20 | 19 17 15 13 11 9 7 5

DEDICATION

*To fellow Augustinian Martin Luther,
father of the German language
and great religious reformer—on the fifth centenary
of the start of the Lutheran reform*

OTHER BOOKS BY GILBERT LUIS R. CENTINA III

NOVELS

Rubrics and Runes
Wages of Sin

POEMS

Recovecos/Crevices
Plus ultra y otros poemas/Plus Ultra and Other Poems
Madre España and Illustrated Love Poems
Diptych/Díptico
Getxo and Other Poems
Triptych and Collected Poems
Somewhen
Glass of Liquid Truths
Our Hidden Galaxette

A NOTE TO THE READER: Filipino and Spanish terms are used throughout the book, and a glossary is found at the end of the book to aid the reader. The Internet links provided in this book are active at the time of printing. However, due to the dynamic nature of the world wide web, the publisher cannot guarantee that there will be no errors and that these links will remain unbroken.

CONTENTS

Dedication | iii
Acknowledgments | ix
Preface | xiii

Introduction | 1
    I.   An Overview | 1
    II.   The Problem | 3
           Statement of the problem | 3
           Purpose of the Study | 4
           Importance of the Study | 4
           Scope and Limitations | 5
           Organization of the Study | 5
    III. Demetillo as a "Religious" Poet Defined | 5
    IV. Review of Related Studies | 7

Chapter 1: No Certain Weather | 8
    I.   Poet in a Time of Darkness | 8
          Starting from Darkness | 8
          Tea-Cup Age | 10
          Death of God | 12
    II.   Rebellious Sonnets | 16
          Stern Father | 16

Contents

              Candled Icon | 18
              Saints and Miracles | 19
              Pious Grandmother | 19
              The Pallid Priest | 21
              God Diminishing | 22
    III.   Signs of the Times | 22
              Maggots of Fear | 22
              Myths of Greece | 25
              Kindness and the Steadfast Mind | 28

Chapter II: La Via | 31
    I.   The Way of the Flesh | 31
              Dissonances | 32
              Not There, Not There | 38
              Harmonies | 42
    II.   The Golden Mean | 48
              Reminiscences | 48
              Part of the Whole | 50
              Awareness of the Present | 53
    III.   Annals of the Forebears | 56
              Barter in Panay | 56
              Flight from Tyranny | 56
              Prophetic Vision | 58
              Religion and Superstition | 59

Chapter III: Masks and Signature | 64
    1.   The Way of Art | 64
              Artists Defined | 64
              Praise of Unstable Men | 70
              Filipino Artists | 76
              God and the Artist | 82
    II.   The Scare-Crow Christ | 85
              Man Diminished | 85

Contents

       Man Struggling | 91
       The Authentic Self | 95

Ricaredo Demetillo | 99

Chapter iv: Lazarus, Troubadour | 100
- i. The City and the Thread of Light | 101
  - The City of Man | 101
  - Sic Transit Gloria Mundi | 105
  - Thread Through the Labyrinth | 108
  - Salvation Is for Everyone | 111
- ii. The Redeemed Life | 112
  - Troubadour of the Lord | 112
  - Grace Baffles the Microscope | 115
  - After Enlightenment | 120

Chapter v: Conclusion | 123

Bibliography | 127

Appendix: Letters of Ricaredo Demetillo | 131

Glossary | 155

Index | 158

ACKNOWLEDGMENTS

I want to thank my niece, Therese Cindy C. Garnado Poulsen, for her valuable assistance in the manuscript preparation. Among other things, she served as my representative in obtaining copyrighted materials of my literary work from the National Library of the Philippines, whose staff was cooperative every step of the way and deserved to be commended for a job well done.

A debt of gratitude is owed to poet Gémino H. Abad and literary critic Alejandrino G. Hufana, my gurus at the University of the Philippines, where this book was first conceived and developed. As my thesis adviser and critic, their honest opinions helped enhance this work as it evolved into its current shape and form.

Many thanks to my Augustinian colleagues at Iglesía del Carmen, Fathers Lauro Rodríguez Mariscal, OSA, and Francisco Pajares Marcos, OSA, for giving me the space I need to write despite our busy work schedule at the parish. I am also eternally grateful to Father Miguel Manrique Aparicio, OSA, God bless his soul, and Father Policarpo Hernández Fernández, OSA. As the then vicar provincial and the then novice master of the Augustinian Vicariate of the Philippines, both men zealously worked hard to nurture my growth as a writer while I was a seminarian in the 1970s. Father, now Bishop Emeritus of Iquitos, Peru, Julián García Centeno, OSA, the then provincial of the Augustinian Province of the Most Holy Name of Jesus of the Philippines, backed their efforts. They pointed me to the footsteps of Augustinian men of letters "through the trail blazed by Andrés de Urdaneta, OSA," the Spanish Basque navigator, who was among the first Augustinian religious missionaries to evangelize the Philippines. They brought my home country into the ambit of Western culture and of great literary traditions.

As I have repeatedly stated in this book, *art is a calvary*, and I would never have made it this far on the creative path without the encouragement and inspiration of many friends along the way.

The selfless support of pure souls has nourished and fortified my priesthood of literature: Augustinian nuns Sister Salome de la Inmaculada Concepción, Mother Ambrosia, Sister Lorenza Gequillana, and Sister Candelaria de la Inmaculada—all of them now in the peace of the Lord.

The fellowship of Estrella D. Alfon, Fred M. Marquez, Francisco S. Tatad, Edith L. Tiempo, Nati Templo Redublo, Luis Cabalquinto, Guillermo Gómez Rivera, María Paz Santos, Alberto S. Florentino, Eric Gamalinda, F. Sionil José, C.M. Vega, Celso Al. Carunungan, Leoncio P. Deriada, Kerima Polotan, Dean Teresita Aportadera, Lucila Hosillos, Paquito Tankiang, Evangeline Pascual, Marcelina Cuadra, Estrella Navales, Amelia I. Valera, Nenita Avanceña, Roger Gernale, Jenny Jota, Alejandro Roces, John Peter Estember, Father Pietro Campos and the late Father Andres R. Arboleda Jr., both of the Society of Saint Paul, and the late poet Federico Licsi Espino Jr. has enriched my journey through life. For that, I thank them all.

In Neguri, I am blessed to count on the support of some of the Basque country's—and Spain's—most creative talents: author José María Alonso Alonso de Linaje and his wife María Ana Romo de Miguel, multimedia artist Vicente Jáuregui, poet Antonio Aguirre, and his sister Marimar. Along with Rafael Saénz de Santa María, as well as his brother Juan and all members of the Grupo de Oración of Iglesía del Carmen, including Jesús Gregorio Serna Ares, they have taken me into their warm embrace not only as a friend but a brother.

I look back with gratitude at my Augustinian formators during my seminary years: Pedro Ferrer Cruz, Tirso Vega Blanco, the late Rodolfo Arreza Milan, Moises Vara, Felix Urrutia Anda, Lester Avestruz Salcedon, Rodolfo Sicio Pingol, and my former seminary rectors, the late Restituto Suárez García and Isacio Rodríguez Rodríguez. This list will not be complete without mentioning Father Santos Abia Polvorosa, OSA, who welcomed me with open arms when I entered the religious life. The following fellow Augustinian friars also have my gratitude: Regino Diez, Rafael López, Marcelino Nieto, and Jerónimo Álvarez, who helped me appreciate the wisdom of Saint Augustine.

My thanks also go to Santiago P. Ezcurra, OSA, who set several hymns I wrote to music, and Father Quentín García, OP, my favorite theology professor at the University of Santo Tomás.

My gratitude also goes to Father Gregorio Liquete, OSA, the Augustinian regional vicar who pleaded with me to accept my assignment at Colegio San Agustín Makati so I "could share my writing talent with the students, the fair hope of the fatherland" and former Augustinian Father General Martin Nolan who in 1984 co-wrote with me the lyrics of the hymn "Freedom Under Grace," set to music by Fray Nicolás Echeverría, OSA, our gift to the then-nascent Augustinian Province of Sto. Niño de Cebu-Philippines.

I am likewise indebted to the father generals who succeeded Father Nolan: Miguel Ángel Orcasitas and Alejandro Moral Antón, who have placed their trust in my integrity as a poet and author. Thanks to retreat master par excellence Father Eugene Tramble, OSA, of the Marylake Shrine of Our Lady of Grace in King City, Ontario, Canada, and to visual artist Father Nicéforo Rojo, OSA, for their hospitality and friendship.

My first volume of poetry, *Our Hidden Galaxette*, first saw print in 1970 when a publisher, Colcol & Co. Publishing in Manila, was convinced by my elder brother Romeo R. Centina to take a chance on a young talent like me. My literary career has never looked back since, thanks to my brother, who is now in a much better place.

I am honored to have collaborated with Janet Frances White on this book. This talented graphic artist has shepherded the production of all my books published in the United States, along with my brother Pierce who contributed his editorial insights. My heartfelt thanks to both.

PREFACE

This book is intended to analyze the poetic works of Ricaredo Demetillo, undoubtedly one of the most gifted poets of the Philippines—and in my mind, the best of his generation. The analysis is made from the standpoint of his *Lazarus, Troubadour,* to clarify the poet as a religious poet *sui generis.* "Religious" is used as a generic term, and religion is taken in the Christian framework that entails Christian morality and considers humanism.

My literary criticism of Demetillo's poetry covers his poetic works from the time he published his first poetry collection in 1956 up to 1976. It was in 1976 when my initial admiration of him as a poet, which began in 1971 when I was still a theology student aspiring for Roman Catholic priesthood, culminated in my writing a thesis on his works as a religious poet. This book is based on that thesis, which I wrote for my Master's degree in Comparative Literature at the University of the Philippines.

Besides his qualities as a superior poet, what attracts me to Demetillo is our joint opposition to clericalism. His voice on this issue deserves to be heard by a wider audience. Pope Francis has denounced clericalism as "evil," according to Vatican Radio. This sense of entitlement makes some clerics feel "superior" and "far from the people" so that "they have no time to hear the poor, the suffering, prisoners, the sick."[1]

To this day, I continue to be against clericalism, informed by my own personal experiences as an Augustinian friar for forty-one years. Clerical-

---

[1] "Pope: Clericalism Distances the People from the Church," *en.radiovaticana.va.* Accessed November 12, 2017. *https://bit.ly/3rW5QpH.*

ism, echoing Pope Francis, is a cancer that gnaws at the very foundations of the Church, and it must be extirpated wherever it is found.

Born in Dumangas, Iloilo, on June 2, 1920,[2] Demetillo studied to be a Protestant preacher at Central Philippines College but abandoned his aspiration to become an ordained minister when he realized his heart lay elsewhere: literature. So he transferred to Silliman University in Dumaguete City, where he completed his BA in English in 1947. On a Rockefeller Fellowship grant, he left for the University of Iowa to study poetry. In Iowa, he earned in 1952 his Master of Fine Arts in English and Creative Writing under the guidance of Paul Engle, a long-term director of the Iowa Writers Workshop, and Robert Lowell, an eminent American poet at the time. He further honed his writing craft under Kenneth Burke at Indiana State University, particularly in literary criticism. At the same time, he also came in contact with noted poets Delmore Schwartz, Allen Tate, and Richard Blackmur.

With an MFA degree under his belt, he returned to the Philippines in 1952, shortly after graduating from Iowa. He taught at Silliman University and moderated *Sands and Coral*, the university's official student publication. In 1955, he relocated to Manila after landing a teaching job at the University of the Philippines, where he became recognized as a significant poet and literary critic. There, he taught literature and humanities until his retirement in 1985. At some point, he was named writer-in-residence by the state university. He continued teaching at the university past retirement as professor emeritus.[3] He died on March 27, 1998.

The idea of writing a literary criticism of Demetillo's religious, poetic works came to me after years of exchanging letters with him. Our correspondence started in the early 1970s and ended only with my regular departures abroad near the end of his life. Demetillo himself has described our snail mail exchanges as contributing to his "well-being."[4]

---

[2] Guerrero, Amadis Ma., "Ricaredo Demetillo: Poet of Panay epics," *Philippines Graphics* magazine online. Accessed October 25, 2022. https://bit.ly/3FgMkMc.

[3] Edilberto N. Alegre and Doreen G. Fernandez (eds.), "Ricaredo Demetillo," *Writers & Their Milieu* (Mandaluyong City: Anvil Publishing, 2012). books.google.com. Accessed October 20, 2017. https://bit.ly/3W1ZYJo.

[4] Ibid.

It is important to remember that this book delves into the religious character, substance, and symbolism in Demetillo's poetry rather than its form or structure. Demetillo, at least publicly, shied away from characterizing his poetic works as religious, seeming instead to emphasize their secular nature, except in the case of *The Scare-Crow Christ*. In an article, he described the book as containing poems "objectifying the poverty and the spiritual confusion" of troubled times in the Philippines in the early 1970s. It was a turbulent period marked by militant student activism in the capital that sparked massive street protests and violence between students and leftist workers on the one hand and the state security forces on the other.

> My poetry has been much influenced by the New Criticism in America, but I do not belong to any school. [It] has been concerned with the following major themes: the rebellion of the young against the conventional values of an overly repressive society; the modern journey of the individual from lostness to wholeness and fullest creativity; the rise and fall of civilization, using the myth of Daedalus in ancient Crete to objectify and evoke the human condition; and the important position of the artists as the bearers and the creators of volumes necessary to the renewal of society.

> To project all these themes, I have used the lyric, the elegiac, the poetic essay, the epic, etc., with relatively good success. Always I have been concerned with the human condition and also celebrated the hierarchy of light. Strongest influences: Homer, Dante, Baudelaire, Dylan Thomas, W.B. Yeats, and Auden, not to mention myths of all sorts, including the Filipino ones.

> My...book *The Scare-Crow Christ* was written mostly during the troubled period of student activism in Manila and contains poems objectifying the poverty and the spiritual confusion of the time. One poem speaks of the indifference of the average man to the welfare of the 'diminished, unfulfilled' man and asks, 'Are you not Judas to his scare-crow Christ?' Still another one pays 'tall tribute to the hardihood of man' that is able to survive the horrors of war in Vietnam and elsewhere. But these new poems are evocations, not propagandistic statements.

> My verse drama *The Heart of Emptiness Is Black*, really a sort of sequel to *Barter in Panay*, deals centrally with the conflict between tribalism and emergent individualism, which may have relevance to the present

situation of the Philippines under martial law [the Philippines was under martial rule from 1972 until 1981]. I chose the drama as a form so that I can be heard by the public, for poetry locally is mostly unheard and unread, if not dead. *The City [and the Thread of Light]* objectifies or evokes the lostness of man in the modern city and the poet's search for any available meaning in the human condition today.[5]

To be sure, Demetillo's writings run the gamut of the human experience, an indisputable fact noted by one of the Philippines' foremost literary critics and a colleague of Demetillo at the University of the Philippines, the late Dean Leopoldo Y. Yabes, when he writes:

> Ricaredo Demetillo's poetry, fiction, and criticism belong to a tradition that is both East and West, and his work is being recognized, though a bit slowly, as a distinct part of the world cultural heritage, a blending of oriental and occidental values. His writings offer a rich mine for the student and the science of culture.
>
> Demetillo deals with a variety of themes: the revolt of youth against oppressive society, the rise and fall of civilizations, the spiritual bankruptcy of language that presages political violence and economic distress, the poet's Dantean/Faustian journey through the morass of living to the higher life. An important work, the poet himself says, "evokes and proclaims the life-forwarding sacrifices of the artists, the 'unstable men,' who are the harbinger of the truths—and values—that invigorate and renew society during critical epochs." Another critic has observed that his early *La Via: A Spiritual Journey* is the most sustained argument in verse in any language by a Filipino.
>
> ...One may discern in the lifework of Demetillo an eloquent argument for the integrity of the artist as both individual human being and as social person. José Garcia Villa, the other major Philippine poet of the twentieth century, maybe patronizing towards Demetillo's social commitments, but Demetillo, while recognizing the superior quality of Villa's personal lyricism, is proud of his stand. Although both Villa and Demetillo accept the centrality of the formal, or aesthetic, values in a work of art, Villa stops there. Demetillo, however, goes further,

---

[5] "Ricaredo Demetillo." Contemporary Poets. *Encyclopedia.com*. Accessed October 19, 2017. *http://www.encyclopedia.com/arts/culture-magazines/demetillo-ricaredo.*

looking for additional values that may enhance the beauty and significance of human life. As a poet Demetillo has attained a stature that in Philippine literature is hard to erode and difficult to surpass.[6]

As a religious poet, Demetillo starts with doubt. After leaving a Protestant seminary in favor of a career in literature, he writes "rebellious" poems because they reject the kind of god society and the institutionalized Church have imposed upon men.

From rebellion, the poet undertakes a spiritual journey that is a flight from wrong values, hypocritical religion, crumbling civilization, and moral corruption. For Demetillo, God is the God of the living, not the dead. Heaven and hell are within man himself; through self-knowledge, man regains his lost paradise. Love alone heals and forgives.

After his spiritual journey, Demetillo finds the immanent God through his kinship with fellow artists. *Art is a calvary; the artist participates in Christ's calvary.* Restless in spirit, the artist can rest in God because he alone can fill the void within the artist's heart. The artist is God's instrument in this world to proclaim and glorify him. Through the life and art of the artist, God is completed in the world of the tangibles.

Gilbert Luis R. Centina III
November 21, 2017
Iglesía del Carmen, Neguri,
Getxo, Biskaia, Spain

---

[6] Ibid.

INTRODUCTION

AN OVERVIEW

Although described by his critics as a religious rebel, Ricaredo Demetillo, in his poetry, has always been concerned with man's relationship with his Creator. His eight volumes of poems—*No Certain Weather, La Via: A Spiritual Journey, Barter in Panay, Daedalus and Other Poems, Masks and Signature, The Scare-Crow Christ, The City and the Thread of Light, Lazarus, Troubadour*—celebrate this interlocking theme that is unique with him.

No Certain Weather navigates between the poet's doubt as he struggles in a "time of darkness" and the poet's hope as he takes things spiritually with "kindness and the steadfast mind" despite being subject to human foibles,

Armed with cynicism, the poet embarks on a spiritual journey, which *La Via* is. In the book, he points an accusing finger at the pre-Vatican II Church: "The sad truth of the matter is that the Christian religion, in its institutionalized form, has been, for millions living in so-called Christian countries, less than the means of leading the fullest life. Its critics claim the Christian Church is itself one of the most formidably repressive agencies of the day."[1]

Daedalus and Other Poems underscores the spiritual quest in the rise and fall of civilization, a kind of religious restlessness, so to speak, even as *Barter in Panay*, for all its allusions to the *anitos*, insinuates the early Filipinos' belief in one Supreme *Bathala*.

---

[1] Ricaredo Demetillo, "Preface," *La Via: A Spiritual Journey* (Quezon City: University of the Philippines Press, 1958), vi.

Masks and Signature, evoking and celebrating the artists who have stirred, often considerably, Demetillo's sensibility, indicates a belief in the immanent God. Spiritual kinship with fellow artists is, of course, a result of the common Christian doctrine that all men are descended from Adam and Eve or, in the light of the New Testament, that the Church is the Mystical Body of Christ. *Masks and Signature* is basically about the healing process, central to grace, both in the artistic and religious sense. *The Scare-Crow Christ* deals with the very poor and the most exploited. Christ is the highest being men can attain, but the ordinary man is a scarecrow in society.[2] This collection, which teems with socially-conscious poems that attempt to project the image of man in its totality, could well be the preparation for the City poems in *The City and the Thread of Light.*

The City and the Thread of Light reminds one of the Augustinian evocation of the city of God in contrast to the city of man, but with a contemporary and native setting. The City poems culminate in San Agustín Church, in Manila's historic district of Spanish-era colonial buildings, and the modern Cultural Center of the Philippines, where the religious and the artistic are unified. In the City poems, Demetillo has written one of his most beautiful poems, "Saint Francis in Ecstasy."[3]

---

[2] "...*The Diliman Review* is publishing my next book: *The Scare-Crow Christ*. The title poem deals with the very poor and most exploited. Christ is the highest men can attain; but in our society, the ordinary man is a scarecrow. You can make your own metaphysical significances, versed as you are in the levels of meanings involved in metaphoric language." (Letter of Ricaredo Demetillo to Gilbert Luis R. Centina III, OSA, dated November 27, 1972, Quezon City.)

[3] Of this poem, Demetillo writes: "I am dedicating this poem of praise to our friendship. For me, it is the poem since I wrote *La Via*, that I have returned in humility and faith to the fold of the Son, Lord of Light and Love, who I here celebrate.

"The basic theme of *La Via* I do not repudiate. But I have, on more mature premises, synthesized my religious and artistic pre-suppositions in a manner aligned to the larger, more comprehensive vision which includes faith and love, as well as beauty, all attributes of God. St. Francis, for me, is the great Troubadour poet; and that's the reason I am using his figure in this poem of faith.

"If *La Via* was over-compensation, inviting hubris, this one poem, with all that will follow it, is restitution." (Letter of Ricaredo Demetillo to Gilbert Luis R. Centina III, OSA, dated February 28, 1973, Quezon City.)

Lazarus, Troubadour is an act of faith. It is a collection of seventy-seven dazzling poems that the poet has written in a span of seven days,[4] a celebration of the redeemed life based on the archetype of Lazarus in the New Testament. He has named this book *Lazarus, Troubadour*, assuming that he whom Jesus raised from the dead is a poet, celebrating his chance to live a second life. In contrast to *La Via*, which contains rebellious attacks on the Church and religious people, this one is entirely lyric affirmation and evocation, the purest songs that have come to birth in Demetillo's pen. Also, the line schemes are mostly varied and highly interesting. Usually, Demetillo's basic form is the iambic pentameter, but there are many unusual variations this time.

Seized by his Creator, the iconoclastic rebel ends his spiritual journey by finding, through Christ, with Christ, in Christ, the Alpha and Omega of Everyman.

II. THE PROBLEM

STATEMENT OF THE PROBLEM. The merit of Demetillo as a poet is not in the poetry of his subject but in the subject of his poetry. In the field of religious verse, Demetillo's poetry is one which we may consider *sui generis* in the best sense of the phrase. He cannot be compared—it would be unfair to do so—with poets in the mystical tradition of Spain like San Juan de la Cruz and Santa Teresa de Ávila, nor with the English metaphysical

---

[4] Regarding this, Demetillo writes: "Sometimes I almost want to cry, because of these seizures of creativity. The last this happened was with *La Via*, in 1958. My long works have been done without this illuminating ecstasy, for instance, *The Heart of Emptiness Is Black*. "Do you believe that there are a few men seized by God? I believe that implicitly. The whole world is transfigured by this experience of Light…I wish San Agustín has plenty of money to publish a work like this, which is to me a gift of the Mysterious." (Letter of Ricaredo Demetillo to Gilbert Luis R. Centina III, OSA, dated September 13, 1973, Quezon City.) Actually, there are around a hundred poems, but the publisher decided to publish only seventy-seven for economic reasons.

poets like John Donne, who was a Catholic, and Andrew Marvell, who was a Protestant. He does not pretend to have the mystical ecstasies of the former. Neither does he choose to identify himself with the latter with their "intellectual emphasis, an emphasis apparent both in the preoccupation of the poet(s) and in their procedure(s)" which lean heavily on the use of conceit,[5] a species of metaphor which both Donne and Marvell used to great effect in their best works. His being a religious poet *sui generis* is perhaps the best virtue of Demetillo as a religious poet within the Christian context. Our problem, therefore, is to discover the spiritual elements in the poetry of Demetillo by treating him as a religious poet *sui generis*.

PURPOSE OF THE STUDY. Our purpose is to explore the theological concepts of Demetillo in his poetic works. It is also our purpose to trace the religious development of his poems since immediately after he had given up the ministry at the outbreak of the Second World War in favor of literature with the publication of *No Certain Weather*, which served as his thesis toward his Master of Fine Arts at the University of Iowa, until the publication of his volume of poems, *Lazarus, Troubadour*, in 1974. This book does not deal with Demetillo's poetic works that came after 1976.

We want to show four periods in the development of Demetillo as a religious poet: 1) a period of religious doubt as attested to by *No Certain Weather*; 2) a period of a religious quest as reflected in *La Via: A Spiritual Journey*, *Barter in Panay*, and *Daedalus and Other Poems*; 3) a period of religious kinship with fellow artists and the ordinary man as mirrored in *Masks and Signature* and *The Scare-Crow Christ*; and 4) a period of religious enlightenment as refracted by *The City and the Thread of Light* and by *Lazarus, Troubadour*.

IMPORTANCE OF THE STUDY. Much has been written by literary critics about the works of Demetillo in the form of brief reviews and commentaries, which, however, do not fully grasp the import of Demetillo's works as a totality. Diversified as they are, written by various critics and commentators multiple times, they are mere scratches on the surface that do not go

---

[5] Helen C. White, *The Metaphysical Poets* (New York: MacMillan and Company, 1935), 74.

beyond the form. Demetillo has not been placed on his proper pedestal, and no study has ever been conducted on him as a religious poet. Our study, then, happens to be the first.

SCOPE AND LIMITATIONS. Our study will be limited to the analysis of *No Certain Weather, La Via: A Spiritual Journey, Barter in Panay, Daedalus and Other Poems, Masks and Signature, The Scare-Crow Christ, The City and the Thread of Light*, and *Lazarus, Troubadour*.

ORGANIZATION OF THE STUDY. Our study is a subject-matter analysis of each poetic work of Demetillo, with a summary at the end of each chapter.

III. DEMETILLO AS A "RELIGIOUS" POET DEFINED

"RELIGIOUS" POET. Demetillo's literary career spanned nearly six decades. He started writing poetry in 1941,[6] although his first volume was published only in 1956, and he continued on this path until he died in 1998. The quality of his books of poetry is of the highest order of consistency, where the subject matter is concerned. He has enlarged his vision with variations on the general evocation of the human condition. Furthermore, as one of the most respected critics of his generation, he based his criticism on the central idea that literature should, at its best, deal with the actual condition of man in society.

In calling Demetillo a religious poet, we are mainly influenced by his book *Lazarus, Troubadour*. "Religious" here is a generic term, and from the standpoint of *Lazarus, Troubadour*, religion is taken in the Christian framework that entails Christian morality and takes humanism into account.

If he has to be complete, religion is the element in life that man cannot do without. The concept of the Supreme Being has always been present in all great pieces of literature. With the awareness of the existence of a Creator comes the journey of the human spirit. "The very fact that these

---

[6] Interview with Ricaredo Demetillo. His earliest poems in *Daedalus and Other Poems* (n.p.: 1961) are dated 1941.

men of different ages have dealt with the same theme (the journey of the human spirit) seems to indicate that every particular age needs to have its spiritual journey written by its particular poets, for it is necessary to the maintenance of the psychic health of that epoch."[7]

Demetillo—recipient of the 1968 Republic Cultural Heritage Award for Literature, the University of the Philippines Golden Jubilee Award for Poetry, the Art Association Award for Criticism, the José Rizal Centennial Award for an essay on Rizal's relevance to the present day, the 1973 Outstanding Sillimanian Award, the 1972-73 Don Carlos Palanca Memorial Awards for English One-Act Play, the 1974-75 Don Carlos Palanca Memorial Awards for English Poetry, the 1985 Southeast Asia Writer's Award, and the 1991 Writer's Union of the Philippines Award—is this one particular poet who is fully prepared to write for this one particular age not only on the journey of the human spirit but also on man's relationship with his Maker and the basic theological virtues of faith, hope, and love.

Demetillo exposes the inutility of false piety and sexual repression in the name of religion. He speaks, as an artist, about God. He serves as a bridge between the Creator and creatures and sings of human weakness as well as human endurance. He also channels pettiness which, if not adequately construed, may be taken as blasphemy but when properly understood according to the standpoint of *Lazarus, Troubadour*, is a mellifluous affirmation of the glorious image of man made in God's own likeness. He sings of the Being that men cannot see but whom they should believe in. To know, to love, and to serve God? Yes. Adoration, praise, expiation, and petition are present in the poetry of Demetillo, just as they are present in the psalms of David. In this regard, Demetillo is a religious poet.

The epithet "religious" disregards the glaring fact that Demetillo is not a religious leader in the sense that he is neither a rabbi nor a minister nor a priest. One does not have to be any of these to be capable of writing religious verses. Although Demetillo has not clearly defined his position on what really is the institutional Church, and although his early works do not really resolve any religious dogma, we base our assertion that he is a religious poet on his work, *Lazarus, Troubadour*, by ordering the chaos and

---

[7] *La Via: A Spiritual Journey*, p.v.

the contradictions expected of a mind that cannot base the life of grace on fears and anxieties. "Man must stand as Son of God with poise and dignity, not slinking by because of his fears and anxieties. Sin is not central to our faith; it is Love that understands, heals, and forgives."[8]

IV. REVIEW OF RELATED STUDIES

Philippine Studies, a journal published by the Jesuit-run Ateneo de Manila University, contains long reviews of *La Via* and *Barter in Panay* by Emmanuel Torres. Felixberto Santos reviewed *Masks and Signature*; another review of the same work by Jolico Cuadra was published by *Solidarity.* Louella Cecilia R. Centina and C. Meng Magno wrote separate reviews of *The City and the Thread of Light* in *Philwomanian* and *Fina,* respectively. We also wrote a review, this time of *Lazarus, Troubadour,* for the *Philippine Collegian.* Perhaps the most interesting reviews, fair and more comprehensive, are those by Leonard Casper in *Solidarity* and his *The Wounded Diamond.* All these reviews, however, do not serve much of our purpose. The authors have limited themselves to either assessing the stature of Demetillo as a poet or superficially discussing his merits and demerits concerning aesthetics.

We did attempt to fully grasp the import of Demetillo's works as a totality through an article, "On the Filipino Poet's Image of Man,"[9] in the *Philippine Priests' Forum.* It is the first of its genre to have come out in this publication intended for priests, and the author is the first to confess that it is wanting in scholarship. Nevertheless, the article has served its purpose: it is actually the genesis of this book. Its limitations and shortcomings have prodded us to undertake the present study, although we are the first to admit that much still remains to be done.

---

[8] Ricaredo Demetillo, *Lazarus, Troubadour* (Quezon City: New Day Publishers, 1974), ix.
[9] Gilbert Luis R. Centina III, OSA, "On a Filipino Poet's Image of Man," *Philippine Priests' Forum,* vol. VI, no. 1 (March 1974), 96-99.

CHAPTER I

NO CERTAIN WEATHER

Religious pessimism and irony dominate the tone of *No Certain Weather*, Demetillo's first published volume of poetry. The poet is undergoing a spiritual crisis when he writes these poems, having left a Protestant seminary in favor of a serious literary career. Thrown into the world to be his father's son again, he has not yet ascertained whether his has been the right choice. His teaching stint at Silliman has proved the way to Iowa. As his father is shaken by the abrupt transition in his state of life, the poet assumes the stance of a religious rebel. He asks theological questions that do not necessarily demand rhetorical answers.

I. POET IN A TIME OF DARKNESS

STARTING FROM DARKNESS. In this trying period of his religious travails, there is no lamp to illuminate him. There are doors, doors, and more doors, but all of them are locked.[1]

---

[1] Ricaredo Demetillo, "Poet in a Time of Darkness," *No Certain Weather* (Quezon City: Guinhalinan Press, 1956), 1. All poems considered in this chapter are to be found in the same work.

> There is no lamp that leads me from this dark,
> Past of door sills to a room. Only the bark
> Of mongrels and the growling darkness starts
> The hackles on my neck, where a black wart
> Now registers the chill. I knock at doors
> But they are locked. Windows are grilled by fear
> Against the brigands of a desperate year....

"Bark of mongrels," "growling darkness," "black wart," "grilled by fear," "brigands of a desperate year"—they assault his senses in the dark as he gropes his way for light.

> It is the month of mocking cuckoos, and the rain
> Falls on the whoring blinds from which a slain
> Moth dangles, stirred by lightning that eerily bares
> A divan mauled up by a naked pair,
> Starting at creak of door or drought of air.
> Drenched by cold shame, I remember that story
> Of sudden death: of Agamemnon's body
> And Clytemnestra's dark incestuous hair.
>
> The shadows warp the rubble of a park
> In monstrous twistings against a timorous dark;
> And on the grass, I see gargoyled lips
> Fixed in the mockery that shrapnel chips:
> A chiseled smile turned into a shapeless howl.
> I stumble on a statue, and my hand
> Uncovers fractured fingers from coarse sand.
> Above me drips the dull hoof of the owl.[2]

Darkness is a veritable wasteland by itself that thrives on the negatives: "whoring blinds," "slain moth," "naked pair," "cold shame," "rubble of a park," "gargoyled lips," "chiseled smile," "shapeless howl," "fractured fingers," "dull hoot of the owl." Agamemnon's body and Clytemnestra's "dark incestuous hair" are a story of "sudden death."

How does the religious poet survive in this valley of nothingness? Demetillo's antidote: "claim this weedy ground, the niggard soil of sense."

---

[2] Ibid.

> I claim this weedy ground, the niggard soil
> Of sense in which few sturdy poems coil.
> I wait beyond this night the farther dawn
> That I may coax fruit from the stubborn stone
> And hew the ruins to another park.
> Even the darkness shapes my shadow, and
> I feel a solid footing where I stand
> Tall in the rubbled warping of the dark.[3]

Perseverance, the religious equivalent of endurance, is of the essence here.

TEA-CUP AGE. Light, even though it passes through darkness, will never be polluted. The poet, especially if he is a religious, cannot afford to be shaped by darkness forever. He has to emerge from his cubicle and be part and parcel of humanity. Observant as he is, he is also a brewer of tempests in this tea-cup age.

> The hedges are correct at Stephen's Road.
> Grass is circumspect, barbed by blades
> Trimming lush plume-tips to precious height.
> Framed by hibiscus, the cottages, all white,
> Screen off the odious insects, though the toad,
> With weary enterprise, may sometimes fright,
> Hopping near beds, intimidating maids.
>
> This is sabbath. Observant, I notice
> Doors open at Stephen's, that the flock,
> Starchy or nyloned, may lap beatitude
> Sipping Christ's blood, the apportioned food
> That made the ancients lean but moderns fat.
> They bleat loud praises to an unctuous god:
> Such is the virtue of the present stock.
>
> Brewer of tempests in a tea-cup age,
> I tramp time here, feeling correctness lames
> In those who plan tomorrow like a meal.

---

[3] Ibid.

> I cannot peg life for a spurious grail,
> And sabbaths cannot calm my tempest's rage.
>
> Pressed to the barbed fence near the church, a frail
> Wolf stares at the proud heels of the pious dames.[4]

In the first stanza, the toad with "weary enterprise" that may sometimes fright, hopping near beds, intimidating maids, calls to mind the whited sepulchers denounced by Jesus Christ. Correct hedges, circumspect grass, and white cottages suggest the passion for the prim and proper. The toad's presence strips off the mask of hypocrisy and exhumes a malady that is more than physical.

The irony is heightened in the second stanza by observing the "starchy or nyloned" congregation. Bleating "loud praises to an unctuous god" makes them sabbath worshipers who specialize in pharisaical utterings and spend the rest of the weekdays reverting to their old vices. Why is "god" not capitalized? In the third and last stanza, the poet hints at the answer in this line: "I cannot peg life for a spurious grail."

In fine, the poet sees these so-called Christians as no better than their pagan counterparts. The Eucharist did make the ancients lean, but it does make the moderns fat. Those who purport to follow Christ use God's name to exploit his people. The sabbath gathering is more of a mundane occasion to display earthly apparel. The sight of a frail-looking wolf staring at the proud heels of the pious dames is another way of re-telling the parable of the beggar Lazarus and the rich Dives.[5] For his part, the poet can only trample time here, being a "brewer of tempests in a tea-cup age."

In the mid-darkness, though, there is a sensual fire that holy ghosts his home.

> The sensual fire that holyghosts my home
> Tongues through the ash of my dissolving years,
> Licking my flesh to ecstasy with flame
> As once it smoldered round my naked fears.

---

[4] "Tempest in a Tea-Cup Age," 2.
[5] Cf. Luke 16:19-31, *The Jerusalem Bible* (London: Darton, Longman & Todd, 1966), 120-21. This is one parable in story form without reference to any historical personage. The rich man is customarily given the name *Dives*, Latin for "rich."

> How the dove flies around my narrowed fire
> To which I'm votary and priest to chant
> The advent of a birth cribbed in my thighs,
> Christ in the groin's shrine whose testament
>
> Is sacred to the blood of boy or girl
> When the green earth cracks to fiery flower.
> See, as I sing, I wreathe continual praise,
> But in this frigid narrow zone, the dour
>
> A envious Pharisee glares that such song
> Be rolled out to the town by lips
> Whose color, still uncrushed by frittering fear,
> Taunts his own veins from which dull passion drips.[6]

"The new-born minute laughs beside the heart" where the poet faces Pandora's box. The morning "proffers sleep like death." To the poet, the dark is "the simulacrum of death."[7] In the finality of it all, man's ego is deflated by his own desire, proof enough that he cannot contend with the Infinite.

> Man, man, that puffed doll shaken by desire
> Loosens at stitches to a shapeless rag
> And who declares a hurricane of dreams,
> Dams up his arteries against the damps
> And cocks crow in his clock though storm-floes blot.[8]

DEATH OF GOD. When the poet comes face to face with the reality that he is mere nothingness, he naturally rebels. He is transformed into Longinus, laughing to see a god that society keeps on crucifying daily.

> I felt like I had seen a god
> Gripped by the bloody nails,
> Who writhed beneath the rod.
> I laughed to see him die.
> But as I trudged home from the hill
> Where the Cross loomed,

---

[6] "The Sensual Fire," 3.
[7] "Pandora's Box," 4.
[8] Ibid., 5.

> A lonely shadow hemmed me in,
> Like shuttered doom.
> Now haunted by the thorny brow
> That I helped pierce,
> I run feeling accurst,
> Pursuit behind.
>
> But every step the shadow gains.
> I faint in dread.
> The dark, shot through with light,
> Reveals the young god's head.[9]

As a rebel, the poet maintains his orthodoxy. The figure of a dead "god" may yet stand for Christ. The Christian teaching that Christ died for humankind is still explicitly affirmed by the line "That I helped pierce." On the other hand, the Old Testament common belief that whoever saw God would die is practically discarded and, to say the least, made fun of. Iconoclast, the poet topples down the myth by laughing it off. The God that society wants to present is reduced to a god. Upon seeing god, the poet does not die. Instead, he lives to witness the death of that god who cannot go farther than hem him in and haunt him as a shadow.

Rebellion is contagious. In his preoccupation with the death of a god, the poet visits a graveyard on a hill where people, most of them living before his time, are buried. The scent is familiar and familial: Uncle Nicolas, whose laughter was thought obscene; Aunt Antonia, who used to walk a prim but palpitating street; and his father, who might have as well represented the dead god.

> Here Father lies, obstructed by a wall
> Of drab concrete from stepping out to troll
> A greeting to the sun.
> I used to see him leap and run.
> Across his fields, sun-dazzled at each eye
> Now he lies dead, in strict conformity.[10]

Here they all lie, part of the parody of the city where the poet is a rebel habitant. How then can the rebel bet on man when he knows "the snouts

---

[9] "Longinus," 6.
[10] "The Graveyard on the Hill," 7.

that, snorting, tear the human morrow"?[11] Once he is in his lush years, he could dogmatize, but age has eroded the bluff of childhood faith. So in this dusk, he peers uncertainty beyond the narrowing orbit drawn by light.[12] If God is not dead, then he must be out of town. Otherwise, how do you explain the existence of a storm? How do you explain an accident? Does God care? Do prayers matter? God should do something. At least he should still the waves.

> What if we sink, will Father rue
> That he should send me out into a gale?
> Does Father care? Why does the heaven let
> A mere cloud bloat, breeding a baleful gale?
> Do monsoons inundate the knoll of prayers?
> But if they don't, then God should still the waves.[13]

Or is God only asleep? We find one instance in the life of Jesus Christ. Christ falls asleep. Suddenly, a storm breaks over the lake, making his disciples panic. When they awaken him, he rebukes them for their little faith. As expected, he calms the storm. The disciples marvel in their minds at the way the waves obey Christ.[14] Demetillo clings to hope, "that buoyant spot on any sea."[15] To faith? God is not dead in Moses.

> Rock sprouted springs when Moses talked,
> And locusts showed the gold clamp of a throne.
> I pause to note the paw of lightning blaze,
> Dashing dark sockets to my house of bone,
> While eunuchs' eyeballs dimmed to a dead glaze.[16]

---

[11] "Poem Written in Balara Park," 10.
[12] "Don Angel," 11.
[13] "The Storm," 14.
[14] Cf. Matthew 8:23 ff.; Mark 4:35-41; Luke 8:22-25.
[15] "The Storm," 14.
[16] "Rock Sprouted Springs," 15. The word "dashing" here is questionable. Perhaps it can be taken as a poetic license, but as it stands, it is a grammatical lapse. The poem has the peculiar strain of Dylan Thomas, which is no longer our concern here. The allusions to Moses do not mention any particular incident, but we can more or less surmise that the poet here is referring to Moses' clash with the obdurate Pharaoh.

The poet is a somnambulist, while we are pariahs to ourselves. "We cross ravines of fear, wrestling with ogres/Our monstrous yearnings have sown like dragon's teeth/And we shrink, appalled, seeking our clanking harvest." The god in whom the poet does not believe is not really the authentic, true God, but the god rammed into his system by his elders, as he confesses in one of his most powerful and most profound indictments of idolatrous myths:

> The god my father chiseled with his tongue
> And shaped within the niche of his child's ears,
> Offering it the chilled dish of my fears,
> On his deathbed was my inheritance.
>
> As in dread shrines, the worshiper turns pale,
> Daring not touch tabooed things lest he die,
> Like Uzza by the Ark-wheels, so did I
> Who lashed myself before it all night long.
>
> It loomed a fearsome thing. Fiercer than Jah,
> Who struck a decalog of stone, the god
> My father willed me held a hissing rod
> That struck me who confused the moral score.
>
> I, like the savage who will dare not strike
> Back at the cobra biting him but not placates
> His fanged tormentor, lifted no hand, but my hate
> Grew for I wished to dash it to the floor.
>
> No cowardice kept back the blasphemy,
> Until a Rabbi whispered in my ears
> The vicious idol toughened on my fears,
> Which if withheld from it, would make it die.
>
> Since then, I kept away the dish, and I
> Have seen my curious heirloom shrink to wood,
> Crumbling to pieces where it once stood,
> A Ba-al that devoured its devotee.[17]

---

[17] "The Vicious Idol," 18.

Darkness, indeed, envelopes the poet. Fear, uncertainty, and scruples result from our false concept of God as an "idol" born of fables and pious exaggerations. We have to destroy this myth if we want to rise above ourselves. Fear must be cast out as we have to be exorcised of false moral values that further alienate us from our God. Is there a Minotaur?

> The fear itself becomes the Minotaur
> That gores or guts.
> We feel the wall close in,
> And if the secret cord frays at the shards,
> Would not the monster trample down the heart?[18]

God is unfairly equated with fire and brimstone. This should not be so. Nameless, faceless fear has no place in one's attempt to know God. Self-knowledge is important—without fear, without self-pity. The poet, now freed from the dogmatic, stifling walls of a seminary, wants to destroy religious myths to be at peace with religious realities, to slay a god to confront the God, and to burn darkness in order to get a glimpse of light. In the poet's own words: "Know that my sly mind mimics God."[19] It is God at last written with a capital G.

II. REBELLIOUS SONNETS

There are six poems included under the heading "Rebellious Sonnets." Each of these poems requires a separate study. We can surmise, after repeated readings of these sonnets, that they represent or, rather, tell the various stages or instances in the poet's life that have contributed to his religious cynicism and seeming loss of faith.

THE STERN FATHER. The figure of the stern father looms tall in the first sonnet. The poet is reduced to a mere child, cowering before a father who delights in giving punishments. Sin has its sadistic reward always; always,

---

[18] "The Victims," 20.
[19] "Life and Death," 24.

disobedience is a sin. God is misrepresented by the father as a despotic judge without any sense of humor, ready to mete out physical punishment at the slightest provocation.

> How could the cowering child believe that God
> Loved and forgave when my stern father, in
> Whose hands the bamboo quivered to a rod,
> Nailed at my side? I felt the straps of sin
> And disobedience, lashing my body raw,
> When sunlight riddled pastures and I ran
> Forgetting furrows and the tyrant hoe
> That blistered hatred in my taut hands.
> God menaced me, and when the text was read
> How Adam, having chewed forbidden fruits,
> Hid in the fearful garden, the ominous tread
> Of judgment creased above me, and I cried.
> The startled audience eddied at my side,
> And father loomed large in his righteous beats.[20]

The sonnet reveals the following: 1) God loves and forgives; 2) sin is punishable; 3) Adam committed original sin by his disobedience; 4) God judges our sins.

"God loved and forgave" may refer to Christ, who came into this world to forgive sins, or to God the Father, who so loved the world that he gave his only-begotten Son, or to both. Demetillo does not specify. The juxtaposition of the bamboo "quivered to a rod," which is "nailed" to his side with the "straps of sin and disobedience" lashing his body raw, produces an ironic effect. All things being equal, the premise that "God loved and forgave" brings out harmful conclusions. Love and forgiveness become a myth of punishment.

Worse still, the poet implies that his father has a hypocritical sense of righteousness. Is it intentional that "Father" in the last line is not capitalized? The child, out of fear for his imagined sin and disobedience, is menaced by god.

In the person of his father, who towers before his guilt-ridden eyes, the child finds religious services on occasions of sorrow emanating from the

---

[20] "Rebellious Sonnets," 26. These sonnets are to be found in *No Certain Weather*.

remorse of conscience. Religion terrifies the sinner and makes the righteous despotic in their stainlessness. Instead of healing, religion maims and alienates the creature from God.

CANDLED ICON. As part of a frayed autobiography of his troubled conscience, the poet recoils how, as a child, he discovers the impotence of a god in a graven image. Grandma's painted icon is too benign to be ignored in times of trouble. As if it were not wood at all. But the child is too precocious for his age. Curiosity topples down the childhood worship of a painted icon.

> Once as a child, I thought God was near
> As Grandma's icon on the leaning wall
> And as benign, for it inclined an ear
> As if it were not wood to listen. All
> My heart reposed beneath its candled feet.
> The palpitating noons, with longing, brought
> Me suppliant, a fugitive from heat.
> Before its presence. In its face I sought
> A surer kindness than what kin or friends
> Could dole me from the hurry of their steps.
> Then God receded, and I felt the fiends
> How in my ears as on the day I tipped
> The icon with a curious finger, and
> I felt ant pellets leak on my shocked child's hands.[21]

Is this shocking discovery really a part of the poet's childhood? There is room for doubt. Demetillo grew up in a Protestant atmosphere, and it is common knowledge that Protestants consider it idolatry to worship a graven image or to make a representation of God in any graven form. One doubts whether Demetillo's attack is leveled at the Protestants. We take this incident, therefore, on the purely literary level, as an unabashed criticism of the practice of making images of God out of wood, so rampant among pre-Vatican II adherents of Roman Catholicism. From Demetillo's words

---

[21] Sonnet 2, 26. The sexual interpretation of this sonnet is the subject of our critical analysis in progress on the sexual elements in the poetry of Demetillo. We take the poem as an episode in a young boy's first masturbatory experience. An erotic film we once saw made use of the movements of a line of ants to dramatize the climax of masturbation.

regarding "Grandma's icon on the leaning wall," we can infer that this encounter probably led him to the Baptist Church, where he was formally baptized at the age of 15.[22]

SAINTS AND MIRACLES. Bureaucracy in the institutionalized Church has also been instrumental in killing the poet's childhood piety. The faithful are duped into thinking that the patron saint will serve as an intercessor. Censers, incense, and the sound of priestly orisons enthrall one for a moment, but when the mystic rapture has been spent, a feeling of loss takes place after pompous religious ceremonies.

> As petty words betray love, it dies
> A slow death, so my childhood piety,
> Directed to a god I thought lived in the high
> Imperious heaven, was betrayed likewise,
> Not once or twice but many. Once in church,
> I doffed my silk red-feathered cap and left
> It on my patron's pedestal, a perch
> Of sacred trust. How should I know a theft,
> Which would rob me doubly, could be done
> Beneath my trusted patron's feet? For I,
> Enthralled by censers, incense, and the sound
> Of priestly orisons, did see no one;
> Until, the mystic rapture spent, my eyes
> Discovered loss. Sobs sowed a bitter ground.[23]

Does this mean that Demetillo does not believe in saints and miracles? This question can be answered by another question: What are those saints doing in the sanctuary? As "heroes" of the Church, they can edify and inspire one to work towards one's sanctification, but it does not necessarily follow that they should be worshiped. Demetillo, in this regard, is very Protestant in outlook.

PIOUS GRANDMOTHER. The note on the author in *Lazarus, Troubadour* supplies this information: "When he was a small boy, a devout grand-

---

[22] "Note on the Author," *Lazarus, Troubadour*, outside back cover.
[23] Sonnet 3, 26-27.

mother taught Ricaredo Demetillo the immemorial prayers of the Christian Church and told him stories out of her store of chivalric romances and fairy tales."[24] The "devout grandmother" has found her niche in one of the sonnets:

> Grandmother, stiff as starchy olive-drab,
> Got knee-corns as a gift from God; for she
> Would rise each morning to rout a cab
> Church-ward, where she wore out her rosary.
> The noon, which brought the laborer to eat
> His brown rice and dried fish, would see her go
> To labor at devotions in the heat
> Until she spent her strength in cramping awe.
> And when the vespers clanged her last Ave,
> Stars trooping singly like pale convent girls
> Out on a pious airing on the street,
> Nun-like, she cautioned narrow paths for me.
> But wayward, I, not heeding, thought of curls
> Blown in my face and slimly tiptoed feet.[25]

It is more out of compassion than out of spite that the poem reminisces on the piety of his grandmother. He recalls his grandmother's rigorous schedule of religious devotion. She is a pre-Vatican II symbol of a pious lady who recites the rosary in the morning, at noon, and during vespers. There is no mention of the Mass and only allusion to a religious procession with the "pale convent girls out on a pious airing on the street." The grandmother fills the days of the grandson with a litany of "don'ts." She is described as "nun-like." When one correlates the pale convent girls with the narrow-minded attitude of the nuns, one is inclined to think that the poet reveals an adverse reaction toward exclusive schools and the unmarried women in the habit who foment false values with their narrow outlook in life. The grandmother's gift from God is well-deserved knee-corns. This is the poet's rejection of false devotion. Wayward according to pious standards, the poet thinks of curls blown in his face and slimly tiptoed feet.

---

[24] *Lazarus, Troubadour,* outside back cover.
[25] Sonnet 4, 7.

He is now a rebel. He has detected the inane fraud. God himself would not have approved of it.

THE PALLID PRIEST. The poet now turns his attention to the parish priest, who is responsible for the oppressive religious ambiance of the town. The flock are misguided, one by religious one, partly because their shepherd is a bore, partly in spite of themselves.

> The town oppressed me, for the pallid priest
> Droned to his flock a decalog of stone
> Which taught decorum to their Sunday best
> And laced the ladies in their corselets of bone.
> I fled the proper streets and chose a path
> Across the frank loose meadow to the lake.
> The silted ripples lapped and cooled my wrath.
> I was a bronzed god bared against the brake.
> Then as I dangled luxuriant on a stone,
> The waters nibbling at my feet, I gave
> Shouts that amazed the birds, one ruby-red.
> Boldly I hurled defiance at the town
> Huddled behind me like an open grave
> Of dull concrete clasping the mannered dead.[26]

There is logic in the narration of the whole situation. The priest is "pallid," as any dead can be. His sermon is a "decalog of stone," another way of saying that it has no life and cannot animate. Lacing the ladies "in corselets of bone" gives them the appearance of mourners at a funeral. The poet flees from this parody of the living dead and returns to Mother Nature's theme. He is god freed from conventions, baring his chest as he savors independence under the auspices of a life-giving element, water. He hurls defiance at the town. For him, the town is like an open grave whose mannered inhabitants are dead. They have killed themselves by surrendering their will to a belief that offers nothing but monotone. They have given up their chance to rise above themselves. There is no improvement in the first place. The church building is the centerpiece of passivity. The priest is responsible for making these people of God a mass of anonymous faces

---

[26] Sonnet 6, 28.

lost in the quagmire of devotion. From dawn to dusk, from the cradle, the town's inhabitants are entombed by their medieval beliefs.

GOD DIMINISHING. What should we worship, then, in this time of darkness? The guardians of faith and morals who have arrogated unto themselves the task of spreading the Gospel, as far as Demetillo is concerned, have failed. The poet turns to knowledge, but it stings. The universe is fecund, but it is a monstrous hollow. Darkness flutters; wise men are guided by a Star. God is there in his firmament, diminishing, if not yet diminished.

> What should we worship in this time of wrath
> When wise men calculate a marvelous Star
> Gutters in Heaven? Who will guide the path
> Of rustics in darkness as the sirens jar
> The jumpy silence? There is no startled hill
> Where dreams are broadcast, brilliant as a host
> That gave utterance to goatherds, till
> The darkness fluttered—none that we can boast.
> We peer the heavens and sea, diminishing,
> That kind god in a fecund universe,
> That monstrous hollow giving planets birth;
> And as we peer, we feel our knowledge sting.
> And siren-warned, we burrow in the earth.[27]

III. SIGNS OF THE TIMES

MAGGOTS OF FEAR. In the title poem, the poet hovers between allusions and actualities, personages and geographies, rites and rituals, ideas and ideologies, rubrics and runes. Uncertainty compels the poet to make use of his knowledge, which in turn breeds the maggots of his fear. The poet deciphers the signs of the times, hoping perhaps that one can unlearn from them.

---

[27] Sonnet 6, 8.

There is no certain weather in the sky
That we should walk without weatherproof,
For Madaket, Manila and the Gulf
Gather a rumor from the dry hot wind
That pygmies all the scare of other gales;
And Kowloon, Suez and Dover blanch to see
The seismographs that register a quake
Which yet may have through the old earth flowers.

Can we escape the brittled threat of words?
Or turn the wired disaster from our door?
We cannot rig a sail and seek the shoal
For there the huddled trees repeat the score
That possibly we too may hear the crash
Which mushrooms briefly in astonished eyes
Before the debris will crumble down on us
Our knowledge breeds the maggots of our fear.
Now as the squall is bruited in the East,
The lama rides the anxious hump of hills,
Leaving the Buddha flanked by butt and jest.
Hadji Mustafa paces in his cell
Mumbling his woe into lobbered fez;
And in a convent Sister Martha starts
A Gloria Patri, but she turns and sees
A soldier leer across the swaggering aisle.

And in the choked ravines of boulevards
Men jostle in and out. The emigrant
Gawks at a pyramid of sweet and thinks
Of tank treads trampling wheat and grapes
Near Prague and Budapest. A shilling change
Clinkers the till; a D.P. cocks an ear
Charmed by that gospel ring. Aid ladies chat
While sirens hoot the bells of Saint Luke's Church.

Children scratch puzzled heads but cram the dates.
Herr Otto clanks his saber and then yawns
As Kaltmann stalks to lectern from hall
To haw upon the Marxian debacle.
Grinning to see a housewife hug the queue,
A grocer hears the wired desk trill, he sags
To hear the bottom gave to gilt-edged stock.
Down in her flat, Madge thinks of fickle Phil.

> And we who pause to hear the weatherman
> Fidget to find the static drowns his voice.
> Plated by chromium which reflects the glare
> Sense is another billboard by the street
> Where crowds mill round and round and wait
> The lifting of the clouds, afraid the next
> Least rap of thunder will release the bolts
> Toppling young David and the Lady's Torch.[28]

Written in the first half of the fifties, the title poem is witness to contemporaneous events at that time, which may no longer ring a bell for the present mind unless one is a student of world history. The mention of Dover to a student of literature is significant. Is Demetillo influenced by the pessimism and cynicism of Matthew Arnold in the poem "Dover Beach"? The mention of the lama riding the "anxious hump of hills, leaving the Buddha flanked by butt and jest" is not only satirical but also ominous, for, in the opening line of the third stanza, there is mention of "the squall [that] is bruited in the East." Hadji Mustafa paces in his cell, and next comes Sister Martha, who starts reciting a doxology but is distracted by a leering soldier across the swaggering aisle. The gerund "swaggering" denotes cockiness, presumption, and boastfulness, and it suggests something obscene when associated with Sister Martha and the leering soldier.

Herr Otto can be any ordinary German of the martial breed. The "Marxian debacle" lampoons the followers of Karl Marx. This is substantiated by the "tank treads trampling wheat and grapes near Prague and Budapest" in the fourth stanza. The poet fears for the future of art and democracy. These fears are expressed through his portentous vision of the statue of David, a famous symbol of art, and the Statue of Liberty, a popular symbol of democracy, being destroyed in a Cold-War era construct of the Apocalypse.

The poet now turns his gaze toward a gentleman of wounds, "whose cough spills in the air with clots of blood," whose eyes "saw startling chatter at church-caves and guilty bulbs muffled in a two-room flat."

---

[28] "No Certain Weather," 29-30.

> Where the spire cranes, he sees mosaic breaks.
> (There Jesus patient under lashes stood.)
> Cursing, he gathers darkness in his eyelids.
> As the spire cranes, bells toll him out of grace.
>
> Stooped in his gait, he walks the muddled streets.
> Their grime and torpor complement his own.
> An urchin's cry beside an alley shakes
> The nervous spring that coils in his bones.
>
> Now in this year shouts whose meanings escape
> Like lizards scurrying in a belfry's chink,
> He stands bare-headed and his outshirt flaps,
> Only a pebble fills his pocket now.[29]

MYTHS OF GREECE. Amid the meaninglessness and emptiness of a confused generation, "darkness still hides a land where nightmares whoop."[30] Margined by darkness, the poet absorbs himself in myths of ancient Greece and sees the vision of Europe crying, feeling the bold tongue lick her foamy thighs. The signs of the times are ululations.

> Beneath the sun, under the perilous blue,
> I feel that prodigies will startle sight,
> And that, like Cadmus, I shall reap
> Heroic harvests sickled in the light.
> On the weathering noon I pore, then sleep:
> Only to hear the Theban women weep.[31]

Born of light, why should he design to let darkness engulf his tribe?

He is Pegasus, "bearing with Heliconian pride dray service and the crow's lice-clutching claws." And he, being a vandal daring to destroy the skull-shaped shrine with Italy hooves, "whining above the rubble in joy, watching the hands of children clap or twine."[32]

---

[29] "Gentleman of Wounds," 32.
[30] "Boddhisatva," 33.
[31] "On Reading the Myths of Greece," 34.
[32] "Pegasus," 36.

He is not bold enough to prey on people's weaknesses, though. The fable of a brave moth happens before his sight, but "wedged by the scrupulous lines of thought, he lets his meal grow cold."[33]

Myths magnify realities and sometimes distort them. Thoughts warmly insinuate on the poet their murmurous flight.[34] Like a Greek lover, the poet philosophizes on the subject of love, declaring that "we must fuse in dazzling sensuous light."

> But will the cunning goldsmith really know
> If gold with other metals may not fuse
> Unless they test the two by fiercest heat,
> And only then conclusion dare deduce?

Demetillo's argument is based on Eros, the Greek concept of love, which is different from Agape, the Christian concept of love that overflows and gives its fullness, not the hunger that cries out from the depth of its own emptiness.[35] But then, Demetillo here only reflects the signs of the times written in the hearts of twentieth-century Christians. The human difference between Creator and creature is this: the latter is incapable of fullest Agape.

His three love songs inspired by Eros are set in a zoo, in a dream, and on a beach, bedecked with imageries that are as sensual as they are concrete.[36] In another poem, he exhorts Cophetua to uncover his bride and drink at her mouth, "the sensual fountain." But he cautions the Egyptian king, "...drink not, your Highness, to surfeit:/For then the feet may fail you. Maintain/The bee's stance at the honeyed onset." When desire grows old,

---

[33] "The Human Difference," 37.

[34] "A Little Argument," 40.

[35] Thomas Merton, *The Living Bread*, (New York, 1956), 71-72, as quoted by Federico Licsi Espino Jr., in "Eros and Agape in Religious Years," in *Burnt Alphabets* (Manila: Pioneer Press, 1969), 36. Espino writes: "Eros, the Greek concept of love, refers to a *shole diapason* of relationships beginning with that of Epimetheus and Pandora as described by Thomas Bulfinch; that of Oedipus and Jocasta as dramatized by Sophocles; that of Hippolita and Delphine as portrayed by Baudelaire; that of Alcibiades and Socrates as revealed by Plato; and that of Plato himself and Socrates, which gave rise to the phrase, Platonic love, to mention a few examples.

[36] Cf. "Love Songs," 41-42.

he tells the king, "Wait for the daedal healings before you strive/To pour your passion into her mold."[37] As we shall also see in the next chapter, the *aurea mediocritas,* the "golden mean" of the Greeks, is the safest way in this age of excesses.

The stars are pale, made luminous by cold and darkness. The religious poet, having seen the sun beneath the boughs of aspen, "must sleep and wake, must sleep, dissolve into a death of sleep."[38] The Blessed Mother, more real than all Greek myths, reads the signs of the times with a smile.

> Maria, in whose womb the Christ-Child kicked,
> Felt at her brow and touched a thought;
> And she, without quite knowing, sought
> The margin of the sky which, pricked
> By starlight, bled crimson like a cross.
> This thought, she touched, this vague presentiment,
> Was fear, yet not quite fear, for while
> Instinctively, her hands moved as she bent
> To where her green womb walled the Child,
> She saw the crimson quiver a rose.
>
> Was there a hand unseen by her had brushed
> The heavens, that the bleeding cross
> Blossomed four-petalled, glowing through the hushed
> Inviolate and secret, like a rose.[39]

The Christian poet is no Greek tragic hero. He sees redemption through the darkness, for "later the heat will fly on heron wings." It is summer again: "Not erudite, the earth still writes/A bold hand with its flourishes of gain./The wind applauds along the slopes of hills." For simple people like the farmers, "heaven opens still, holds oracles,/prompts, punishes, is a house of certain doors."[40] For the poet, "morning is a flame-tree in the grove of weather."[41] Life and death are treated more profoundly than in

---

[37] "Cophetua, Uncover Your Bride," 43.
[38] "Shrivelling Autumn," 44.
[39] "Maria, Madre," 45.
[40] "Summer," 47.
[41] "Nature Song," 48.

Greek myths. Resurrection is inevitable for a dead lover who had loved the earth with a strong love. The signs of the times, no matter how dark the walls, are fraught with religious meanings.

> We could not salvage breath, but we could swathe
> His body and lay it in the earth he loved.
> He may return and beckon from a sheaf.[42]

KINDNESS AND THE STEADFAST MIND. The scene is a garden in Carthage, North Africa, around AD 246. At that time, Christianity is gaining tremendous ground despite stiff opposition from some quarters. Saint Cyprian is writing to a convert named Donatus, conscious of the human predicament, of the growing weaknesses of the Roman Empire threatened by the restless barbarians from the North, and of the people's indifference to the signs of the times, the danger very close at hand. Now the setting has become Manila or any city anywhere! The spiritual conditions vary very little.

> Foresuffer all, Donatus; reality is stern
> And they who look into its chasm, reel
> Or even faint. But since we wish to drink
> Stuff stronger than the milk of puking babes,
> Free of the bibs and rattles which the mob
> Must own to tickle and amuse themselves,
> Foresuffer all, and then enrich the soil
> Of hours with kindness and the steadfast mind.[43]

This seems a cheerful world on the surface: birds sing, the winds are warm, and the scent of orange blossoms fills the air. On closer inspection, however, the City is like a lolling woman with half-closed eyes. Sensuality stinks everywhere: the women pray prostrate by night and stake their maidenheads for offering among the trees; the old seek their lairs beside the quay where caravels unload the galley slaves; the young join the crowds among the groves to chant voluptuous hymns to Pan. This is a holiday: the empire is engrossed in its gory amphitheater, prosperity eats up the villas,

---

[42] "The Lover's Death," 49.

[43] "Sand and the Lolling City," 57. Written while the poet was alone as a student in Iowa in the 1950s, this poem is actually the first of Demetillo's City poems.

and men lack the power to oar no matter how they try.[44] The poet is a religious seer who reads the portents.

> And now the comet glory of our age
> Sputters in darkness which usurps the sky.
> The stem of myths on which the gods are reared,
> Like buds on trees, now slowly shrivels out.
> Rome, Carthage, Athens–all will be but names
> To steer the schoolboy's fancy and bemoor
> The balding scholar on a pebbly beach
> Where shadows lengthen as the sun leans down.[45]

Saint Cyprian urges Donatus to do the same.

> Now that the wintry specter shadows us,
> We who are gardeners assigned to till
> The fields, the bonds of which are farthest islands,
> Should read each wary sign nor need we fear....[46]

At this hour of impending doom, Saint Cyprian is resigned to the will of God. It is the religious poet speaking.

> ...And if that night,
> That long, cold night, will follow on the heels
> Of hoarfrost, we sir, may also watch
> Dove wings, like boreal fires, blaze up the sky.[47]

No amount of darkness can eclipse the will to survive. Hope summons faith; faith brings about redemption. There is no certain weather in the sky; the poet's message is clear, but do not despair. "Foresuffer all, and then enrich the soil of hours with kindness and the steadfast mind." This is all man needs to survive the elements that can obstruct his journey toward fulfillment. The journey is about to begin.

---

[44] Ibid., *passim.*
[45] Ibid., 57.
[46] Ibid. The use of "and" instead of "nor" in the last line would have sounded better.
[47] Ibid., 58.

The spiritual crisis in Demetillo's life should be considered when one attempts to analyze *No Certain Weather*, his earliest volume of poetry. The poems included here are written in times of storm and drang in the poet's younger days: at eighteen, he enters a Baptist seminary only to abandon his calling during the war in favor of a serious literary career; he gains his bachelor's degree in English and Literature at Silliman and becomes a teacher after the war. During this time, he leaves for the United States on a fellowship grant in creative writing at Iowa State University, where he studies under Robert Lowell and Paul Engle. Still, he has not truly found his spiritual fulfillment.

This chapter has been devoted to a volume of Demetillo's poetry during those trying years. We have divided it into three parts, further subdivided to follow a logical scheme.

In the final part, we established Demetillo as a religious poet by discussing his "dark night of the soul," and his reaction to a tea-cup age, his unbelief against the dead god that society flaunts.

In the second part, we discussed the six rebellious sonnets, autobiographical in many aspects, which chronicle how the poet "lost" his faith.

In the third part, we reproduced the title poem in full. We have already foreshadowed Eros, the Greek concept of love, which will be discussed again in the next chapter. The poet is pictured as a seer who exhorts his reader to face reality with kindness and a steadfast mind.

CHAPTER II

LA VIA

The journey of the human spirit is the common theme of *La Via, Daedalus and Other Poems*, and *Barter in Panay*. We will discuss this kind of journey in this chapter, which has also been the theme in Homer's *Odyssey*, Dante's *Divina Commedia*, Goethe's *Faust*, and Melville's *Moby Dick*. "The very fact," Ricaredo Demetillo writes in his preface to *La Via*, "that these men of different ages have dealt with the same theme seems to indicate that every age needs to have its spiritual journey written by its particular poet, for it is necessary to the maintenance of the psychic health of the epoch."[1]

I. THE WAY OF THE FLESH

Demetillo admits that the twentieth-century mind cannot write of that journey of the human spirit in the heroic terms of Homer or in the speculative symbols of Dante. While the psychic experience remains basically the same, the external circumstances change; therefore, the mode of treatment will be different. What, then, is the one mode of perception that,

---

[1] *La Via: A Spiritual Journey*, p. v.

more than any other in our time, seems fitted to achieve a confrontation of our human situation concerning the psyche? Demetillo has a ready answer:

> ...that which is provided by depth psychology, just as in Dante's day it was provided by the philosophy of Thomas Aquinas. But this mode of perception is to be reinforced by other modes—the mode of intense self-examination, the mode of satire, irony and wit to achieve critical distance toward the subject; and the mode of symbolic correspondence, from the banal and stupid to the divine, can be forced into exalting consort.[2]

DISSONANCES. The voices speaking in the first book of *La Via* are dissonant. The poet ranges through the present time and the present place. He is confronted by the boring superficialities without end and the abysmal emptiness within. Everywhere he is assaulted by shrill and off-key voices of the damned caught in their web of meaninglessness, horror, and frustration. The in-grown contortions objectify the drought that blights human life everywhere.

The true state of hell is the inability to love and to respond to love. Demetillo has managed to put into the following poem some of the intense sorrow that people feel, within the family circle, when they are incapable of responding to or giving love.

> Young mistress, forsake, heave a sigh,
> Then seek the solace of a chicken pie
> Or hunt a new friend with the telephone
> Or, failing that, try to radiophone.
>
> Having prepared his farewell letter,
> The bankrupt shoots his worries
> With a .32 revolver.
> The worries splatter on the floor.
>
> A husband comes back to his flat
> And finds his wife has flown.

---

[2] Ibid.

> And makes a noose out of his thoughts
> And goes off with a groan.
>
> Veloso wraps his anguish
> In poems scrawled like a sibyl's scrawl.
> But feeling in himself the intolerable pains,
> He slashes his relief, the shrinking veins.
>
> Once in a nurturing time,
> Men knew a provident sky.
> Now that we soar so high
> We find a vacuum there.[3]

Man in our society is spiritually zero, but he does not know it. He does not know himself. He invents gadgets to help him forget life's meaninglessness, but they are useless. The silence of a room is a nuisance to his consciousness, and he prefers to get lost in the noise.

> We cannot stand the silence of a room;
> So, we turn the radio till it drowns
> The shrill insistence, like a caterwaul,
> That we are bankrupt to the very soul.[4]

While the theme of *La Via* is the journey of the human spirit, it points an accusing finger at the pre-Vatican II Church. "The sad truth of the matter is that the Christian religion, in its institutionalized form, has been, for millions living in so-called Christian countries, less than the means of leading the fullest life. Its critics claim that the Christian Church is itself one of the most formidably repressive agencies of our day."[5] Men like to doubt the veracity of religion.

> Men like to feel the Way is all a lie,
> A cassocked one's concoction.

---

[3] Ibid., I, 3. All poems considered in this sub-section are to be found in Book I of the same work.
[4] Ibid., 4.
[5] Ibid., vi.

> Some think it all a sad mistake
> That all guidebooks mention it at all.[6]

The Church to Demetillo is out of step with the times, and suffering as a discipline is outmoded. One merely pops a pill or dresses up for cocktails at the lounge to escape the pain. He or she may feel a little jaded or squalid, perhaps, but not from any sin.[7]

With a macabre sense of humor, Demetillo describes the behavior of his neighbors who profess to be Christians. Mrs. Octavia wears the latest fashion, which all the ladies say is unbecoming, although someone whispers that there is little difference between the matron and a sack of Naric rice. Then there is Mrs. Belmonte, who raves about her house. She expects to land on the society pages of the newspapers; otherwise, it will be a shame. Her advice to her children is not to read as much to avoid being the worst kind of a bore. She is off with her family to Baguio City, the summer capital of the Philippines, every April; in December, they winter in Japan. Her husband is earning enough at the government agency tasked with import control. And the men, gathered in a poker game, talk about exciting topics like the hot real estate market and the latest burlesque show in town. The poet is advised to pursue a career in the insurance industry or public relations instead of sticking it out in the academe, a polite way of saying from supposed Christians that it does not pay to be a teacher.[8]

The Knight of Columbus is a means for social climbing:

> One must, of course, have the right connections,
> Earthly or heavenly.
> It will not hurt our old career at all
> If we should be a KC,
> Or if some think that it is a limitation.
> Then go to church on Sunday
> And have our picture taken
> Chatting with Bishop Yap or Monsignor Vagnozzi.
> We'll kneel before the altar, quite cherubic,

---

[6] Ibid., 5.
[7] Ibid.
[8] Ibid., 6-8.

> Though we sag now about the pelvis regions
> For we have gone to all the choice
> Fleshpots to have our little spree
> In song, in wine and women—
> For we're no saints, as anyone can see.[9]

The Christian youth of the country are miseducated, and they lap up pop culture and foreign values that render them very superficial in their knowledge. Demetillo blames diploma mills for contributing to this deplorable situation; in these business-oriented colleges, students are at the mercy of enterprising professors who sell seminars to spread outdated knowledge. The prodigy of this generation is dangerous to the purse.

> The students of this age are right–
> They chew on comics for their diet.
> Do not say this is asinine;
> The comics *are* American
> And stimulates like rock-and-roll
> To rear our doughty superman,
> Whose accent, curious like his soul,
> Fractures King's English to a fright.
>
> No doubt, he thrives on seminars
> Based on some antique notes, which our
> Professors peddle by the hour
> In downtown colleges or bars.
> What intellectual probity
> Shines on his forehead like a star.
> Oh, when we meet this prodigy
> By all means let us watch our purse.[10]

The Christian lady is devout. She is also a busybody who confuses piety with superstitious awe, passes gossip from house to house, and destroys the name of other people. She is a member of the parish choir, and she regularly goes to confession. Still a virgin, she is both frigid and unkissed.

---

[9] Ibid., 11.
[10] Ibid., 13.

> Waspish of breed and ever ready
> To confuse piety with superstitious awe,
>
> Our neighbor's daughter, reputed a lady,
> Botches good names or slices them in two.
>
> By grapevine or telepathy
> She harvests items that invariably startle.
> With retailer's instincts she imparts them slyly
> To replenish the needs of our good townspeople.
>
> She sings in the choir and goes to confession.
> The priest speaks of her as a true exemplar.
> This much is to her credit: she is still a virgin.
> But I would not care to even kiss her.[11]

Society has laid the ground for the tinsel and tin and the chromed façade. The metropolis is a chaotic marketplace where thieves, beggars, peddlers, and devotees, parody life by mixing the sacred with the profane.

> The virgin soars, borne on a cloud
> Wafted by angels with their melody.
> From a ghesso heaven, the Paraclete
> Streams downward. A devotee
> Grovels before Christ's lacerated feet.[12]

The Nazarene staggers while flagellants lash at the lack of faith. The priest breaks the Bread, the Body of Christ. Miserere downs the angel's song. The present generation is sick, and its casualty list is "impressive." There are those with talents as sharp as razor blades but much dulled by living. What of our ancestors who dreamed of paradise?

> Our fathers moved in forlorn caves
> And though the shadow that beset
> Them was man's fate. Some did not even grieve
> To feel the shackles dragging at their feet.
> Or if they grieved, they were afraid

---

[11] Ibid., 16.
[12] Ibid,, 18. An echo of T.S. Eliot's "Sunday Morning Service"?

The lash would stress their servitude,
So kept their silence and betrayed
The dream of freedom with acquiescent mood.

Did they not kiss the hands that kept
Them captive in that awful cave?
Our fathers penitently wept
Before heir jailers who spurned them like a knave.

Their paddled children had addled brains
And learned to serve the conqueror,
Who booted them to reward their pains.
Submit, submit—this was their chieftest lore.

Not to inquire but to kneel down
And to accept authority—
Our hand-dog fathers felt the frown
Numbing the nerve-ends of liberty.

So, for centuries, they groped—
Light but a glimmer in the cave.
Our fathers perished as they moped
Their fears and ignorance dug out of their graves.[13]

From their *conquistadores*, our forefathers had learned to play the hypocrite, to phrase sly flatteries, to dissimulate. They licked the hands holding the crucifix and appeared as their rabid hate. Our generation is left with its legacy of intellectual and spiritual slavery, and we stretch our joints and blink in the blinding glare of new times.[14] Identity lost, we act the part of a clown: "We are in this together, you and I,/Clowns both, with button eyes and bulbous grin...."[15] The code of morality enslaves the flesh. Rectitude oppresses "...I am well brought up, my parents strict,/Who prayed that I should never be led astray/But walk the narrow path of rectitude/Why should I yield to furtive lusts?"[16]

Agape and Eros are constantly at war with each other in all directions because man finds it hard to reconcile the two factions in his body. The

---

[13] Ibid., 23.
[14] Ibid., 24.
[15] Ibid., 29.
[16] Ibid., 33.

spirit is willing to settle for Agape, but the will is too weak to eschew Eros. Dissonances ramble everywhere: newly–married couples unable to consummate the sex act during the first night; husband and wife remaining so in name only because of a piece of legal paper; gentlemen driven to madness and sexual assaults due to strict sexual conventions. Gone is the paradise where a man was free to roam and take his pick of things. What bars man from reentering it is a flaming sword of guilt.

> Pursued by guilt, out of that innocence.
> Young Adam fled. Pale Eve was by his side.
> The serpent followed them and mocked their thighs
> And discord flared to hate between these two.
> Gone was the paradise that they had shared.[17]

NOT THERE, NOT THERE. In the purgatory section of *La Via*, which comprises the second book, the poet wishes to be free of entanglements, snarling him with other people in the open streets. He finds, as he did in the hell section that, for many, the Church is no longer a good place of refuge for the troubled and burdened because, to them, it is overly stern, unsympathetic, hostile, and unloving. He discovers that to arrive at self-fulfillment, he must pass the same way he wants to avoid. Yet, in the process, he reconciles Eros with Agape and arrives at his original innocence.

With the commission of original sin, the world can no longer act as a womb to cuddle man or give him fetal nourishment. It has ceased to be an Eden where life wafts on the scented wind through a providential wood. Innocence is gone; the winding way is rough. The poet, though, is too proud to depend on a god.

> Once in the innocent paths my childhood knew,
> I heard the footsteps of the genial god.
>
> I plucked pure nourishment from every bough
> And rued no seed that brambled in my blood.
> Now every bramble bunches to a rod
> To lacerate the flesh. Even the ground

---

[17] Ibid., 50.

> We tread is niggard and the boughs are gaunt.
> But I have begged no favors of that god,
> Whose constant mercy bays me like a hound.
> Too proud, I spit the waters of his fount.[18]

In this journey through the dark woods, his fellow mortals join the poet. Some seek comfort in unburdening themselves at the confessionals, while others cannot find a way to ease suffering.

> They cannot find the strings or cord
> To serve as clue to free
> Their feet snarled inexorably
> In the lair of the labyrinth;
> So, go out by the door they came
> Heavier of step, more numb,
> The World within a father surrogate,
> To them a stupid mother....[19]

The Church is too steeped in its old ways, too stern to understand, too frigid perhaps to care, not even bothering to see that sinning may be striving, as abscesses do serve to warn of inflammation.

> Armed with a thou-shall–not,
> The moralist is stern.
> He looks around to spot a heresy
> Or for a sin to burn.
> He fiercely scouts the obvious
> Is often blind to what's within,
> Which often is more odious
> Than any open sin;
> Hence, without intending, he
> Feeds the hog, hypocrisy.
> How can he ever see
> The world's a hospital
> Where sinners heal for free
> The sinner and heretical?
> Or know that he, the Pharisee,

---

[18] Ibid., 59. An echo of Francis Thompson's "The Hound of Heaven"? All poems considered in this sub-section are to be found in Book II of *La Via*.

[19] Ibid., 66.

> Is sick like any sinner
> Since he is spraddled by the sharp split
> Between the flesh and spirit,
> And he is crucified
> By passion? So-called ideals now divide
> Body and soul in a war that knows,
> For Christians, no respite or truce.
> What if the prurience of our day
> And all the violence:
> That in the news and magazines,
> That in the books, the ads and such,
> Maybe the symptoms that the sins
> We try so hard to smother, bray
> Like asses in the church?
> For what's repressed will, in our dreams,
> Turn to a nightmare or a scream;
> For sex denied, hence warped, may rape
> Coarse horror in a human shape.[20]

As critic Dean Leopoldo Y. Yabes puts it:

> The significance of *La Via* is that it presents an approach to the attainment of happiness not through asceticism or mortification of the flesh, but through the proper exercise of the psychosomatic functions of the body. It may be recalled here that the spiritual bliss attained by the poet in *Divina Commedia* was based on an earthly love. So the poet in *La Via* believes that it is wrong to starve the flesh because doing so could lead to crimes of lust and even of simony, since repression of the natural functioning of the body does not make for a healthy and harmonious development of the several faculties of man.[21]

After the sword has come to the cross, men struggle only to gain chastened heaven. As billboards entice people with promises of secrets to gain entrance to heaven, the guilty, the fearful, and the doubtful drag their respective burdens. The proliferation of religious sects, claiming to be the right way to truth, only breeds confusion, and searching for the true way leads to nowhere.

---

[20] Ibid., 67. Most of the poems in *La Via* degenerate into prose, like this one.
[21] "Introduction," *La Via: A Spiritual Journey*, iii.

> Here we are caught, confused by the voices
> That cry, " I am the door to the Truth,"
> But when we follow them, those voices
> Lead to no truth, but all our youth
> Is frittered in the search that may not end
> Save in the dead–end of a city street,
> Where stinks bloom almost palpably
> Beneath the billboards hiding out the tree.
> There we are trapped by trampling feet
> Of those who like us rush about,
> Dissatisfied with uncertain certainties
> Burdened by guilts, or fears, or doubts.[22]

Shall the traveler turn back to search the pews? But why do pilgrims hesitate before the entrance, then disperse, saying it is of no use? Why do they feel as aliens do on coming ashore? Where is the mystery encountered in childhood?

The Church harbors people who think they can buy heaven and are licensed to sin again and again after paying up their religious dues. The Virgin drifts, unmoved by human woes.

> Most who invest their tithes in churches
> And intone a creed that cramps their souls,
> Go out complacent by the door,
> Put by the veil and rosary
> Then hail a taxi home
> To pile up venial sins another day.
>
> How can they know the Jewel is not there,
> The Light that blazed out on a lonely hill
> Consuming dross to make one consummate,
> But must be sought beyond the churches
> Where services are so correct and dull
> And devotees kiss black nazarenes;
> Where tepid pieties are droned in corners
> And drab concrete keeps out the sun,
> While far above the sweat and rabble
> The Virgin soars, borne on a cloud,

---

[22] *La Via: A Spiritual Journey,* 17, 83.

> Ecstatic, unaware of trouble
> Tensing the faces in the crowd.[23]

Christ is gone from the Church and may be found beyond the confines of the physical churches.

Lonely trails are benighted. Where may the traveler turn? There are no landmarks, and the guidebooks are of no help. One must run his gauntlet alone and be glad if the bread crust will not sour if there is a water fountain to quench one's thirst. With nothing to judge oneself by–no Southern Cross, no Polaris–the Church is peopled with moralists whose primary concern is mortal sin and who teach religion for a fee. One has to undergo his spiritual purgatory all by himself. The way out is in original innocence. To go through the labyrinthine passage, one has to be born again.

> The reason wavers here, a lamp that wavers in faint air,
> Then fizzles out and leaves strange darkness on our shore,
> The frantic crutch surrendered to the stones
> That we may cast self on a mercy not of men
> And in our darkness feel the rush of sudden wings
> And see the borealis, that marvel to men's sense,
> Flaming with glory all natural and human things.
> Now, we shall rest like children in that innocence.[24]

HARMONIES. The last book of *La Via* is the heaven section. The poet arrives at self-knowledge and is life-forgiven. Through the mystery of love, he achieves the strength to order his life and is aligned with the creative forces of the universe. Reconciling Eros with Agape, the poet learns to affirm and assert himself. The poet bursts into the exultation of sanative mysteries.

As one of the discussants during the 1976 U.P. Writers Summer Workshop, Demetillo said, "the poet must add something meaningful to human experience by bringing order to a disorderly environment."[25] This is precisely what he has done in the heaven section of *La Via*. In the chaos of his environment, he puts his emotions into order through resolves born

---

[23] Ibid., 85.
[24] Ibid., 87.
[25] Cf. R.V. Pineda, "Writers Draw Battle Lines," *U.P. Newsletter* (May 3, 1976), 6.

out of love. "So, at the journey's end,/We learn humility anew. We kneel before truth cradled in the homely fact."[26]

Magdalene symbolizes repentance in a place where forgiveness rewards one who repents.

> I know why the Christ
> Looked at the Magdalene
> Finding no word to cast
> And bruise her with its stone.
>
> He plumbed the hurt which turned
> Her backward look to salt,
> Sensed desperate walls close in
> To flatten flesh and bone.
> Glaring with sterile sand,
> Her soul's geography
> Sucked at the sensual moisture and,
> Still craving, sapped life's tree.
>
> Such was the blasphemy
> Which writhed from her loose hair
> That men turned fatally
> And hardened at the stare.
>
> Christ looked at the Magdalene
> And she was life-forgiven.
> She felt the climb of sap
> Into each withering vein.[27]

In the preceding poem, Demetillo affirms the godhood of Christ. He is God, and he has the power to forgive sins. Moreover, no sin is too great for God's mercy if the sinner truly repents. Self-knowledge has taught the poet to realize that, after the Fall, it is man who runs away from God. Now tainted, it is man who puts to rout the last of Gabriel's angels from the firmament of self with his atom of disobedience to God's love. An arbitrary

---

[26] *La Via*, III, 92. Appears under the title "The Three Kings," in Asuncion David-Maramba, ed., *Philippine Contemporary Literature*, 4th edition (Manila: Bookmark, 1974), 248-50. All poems considered in this sub-section are to be found in Book III of *La Via*.
[27] Ibid., 93.

need has become a sterner God. The machine has diverted the creature's attention from his Creator.

> Men feel doubtless orphaned and a slave
> To arbitrary need, a sterner god
> That ever greedily lapped the paschal blood
> That dripped between the fingers of the priests.
>
> Men turn away from the confessional
> Seeking purgation in an aspiring
> And every poet, desperate for myth,
> Seeks sleek proportion in a fierce machine.[28]

Christ lived in an age when God forgave. Man must be aware of this and try to know himself, and he must recognize Christ's power to forgive to merit happiness.

The poet gathers his senses which have swooned to their death. From vertigo, they perk up as in blazing dawn. Love stays from temptation—from the Calypsos of doubt and the Circes of despair. Love prevents him from drowning. He cannot explain why, but he is reverent before this mystery of love and living. He could have rebelled forever, but love is firm, gentle, and patient with his ways. Love has shown itself to him as the force moving and keeping the starry galaxies in space, thus teaching him to believe once more.

> I found it is the very law that heals
> The rot and fever of the skeleton.
> I was death's dunce before I learned to feel
> Love's accents rousing corpses in my bone.[29]

Love has become the poet's North Star, making him feel the strange beauty of space once again. Besides being a shrine in the poet's head, quickening like light and air, love is nourishment, like bread. Finally, love sets man free.

> So, I survey my garden like a Lord.
> O miracle, that as I tread again

---

[28] Ibid., 94.
[29] Ibid., 105.

> Among these lanes where once I fled the sword
> That banished me to a wilderness of pain,
> The fallows sprout, grain wakened by glad rain...[30]

Here, in this garden of love, the poet shall belabor—tending to the planets, sending the living Logos his lips form in the freedom of praise-walled haunts. Grateful and awed, the poet is a new Adam awakened from his unbelief, able to praise the Lord of the living.

> I raise these rimes to praise the Living Lord,
> Whose burgeoning touch has roused my nerves and veins,
> Once withered by the drouth that was my death,
> But now I exult, rich with sweet-sapped Word.
> Joy surges like a fecund drowse of rain
> On fields where grass had dried, funeral wreath.
>
> Not to the Nazarene, the lord of death,
> Who cramps his devotees with dark, dull creeds,
> I build this hymn but to the Lord of health
> Whose radiance warms the ardor of my faith;
> For it is He whose fingers cuddle seed,
> Who marches out man's gold, lost in loathed filth.
>
> For if our guilt in thou-shalt-not,
> Worms havoc on the heart, its poison breeds
> Such malice as would curse the sexual tree,
> Then drape a mean leaf on our beggar's lot
> And clamp exile on us among gaunt weeds,
> Where we shall claw for roots–frigidity.
>
> There from that furtive covering of weeds,
> We stalk our Abel with his fertile fruits, for we
> Are also Cain, whose curse now scars our brow.
> Pursued, we snatch our filch to gorge our needs,
> Then skulk, pariah, through the leafless trees,
> Blackened to stumps, clawed by cow-cursed crows.
> Where but in us all the hell we know?
> For as we lurch in drunken insolence
> Across deracinated patterns of a street,
> We see on all the faces that we meet the woe

---

[30] Ibid., 111.

> Which leech-like seeks our cheeks and blights our sense.
> I, Adam, in the run and leap of days,
> Walk in this paradise, reclaimed from tares
> By Love, whose radiant miracles she wrought in me.
> I resurrect upon my lips this praise
> That overbrims and moves the orphic air
> And sways to eloquence and hymning tree.[31]

The hymn celebrates the following: 1) God is the God of the living, not of the dead; 2) guilt, magnified by countless prohibitions, does more damage to many; 3) heaven and hell can be within man himself; 4) man can regain his lost paradise through self-knowledge; 5) love heals.

Once it is in his possession, God clasps the soul, and he moves inside the mansion of the mind, for he is pure spirit. When God rules the body, sacred to his use, he makes man a partner in his creative enterprise. For this reason, the poet celebrates the proper use of the body, for flesh denied exacts its own penalty.

> When starved, this body—ill-shaped flesh and bones—
> Prowls like a mongrel for a garbage can
> And snarls at curs that would possess its bone.
> Along the ridges of its ribs, we scan
> Death's trade-mark, outline of a skeleton.[32]

The poet sees the spirit as "but the body seen/Within each man, a stretch of a country, fair/Or arid, ored with precious stones or mean,/Land rich of soil or miasmal, foul of air/When all is warped or withered by rude glare." The mind "contains a grove where my Lord walks,/His thread of light bright in that sanctuary./There I would wait amazed to hear His talk/Or pluck a jade-bloom from its jeweled stalk."[33]

To the mind that has spiritualized itself, the Paraclete descends, the unparochial Bird, Giver of life, the third Person of the Trinity that renews the face of the earth and makes of man its living temple.

---

[31] Ibid.
[32] Ibid., 113-114.
[33] Ibid., 116.

> The Paraclete, the unparochial Bird,
> Whose descent in a time of avalanche
> Shook down a feather shining on my daze
> And cooed in longing near my panicked heart,
> Now builds its cote and flutters in my grave.
>
> And of its notes, I build this hymn to house
> The Lord, whose coming down to a trumpet blast
> Will wake the host camped near the maggot's claws,
> To sing with cherubims choired in a cloud
> And signal stars to start a three-part rouse.
> All my manhood's cares, once dry with drouth,
> Quickened by rain and love, cradle the seed.
> Trees bend to fruit, and in my half-way house,
> Host of the Light that in my heart resides,
> Praise is a young vine tendrilled at my mouth.[34]

A new day has come; the Word has shattered the awful tomb of unbelief. With the Holy Spirit, Truth is attained. Man sees again the radiant limbs unswathed by pain. Eros now collaborates with Agape as love reconciles law and desire. The poet intones a song to the Virgin Mary, the begetter of gods and poetry. Prudery and falsehood must be consigned to the gloom.

> And now, O Lady, please put off
> The dark robe, dolorous and rough!
> Bare now your naked majesty,
> Begetter of gods and poetry!
>
> Begetter of men and of high myth
> Begetter of the radiant faith,
> Consign all falseness to the gloom,
> Seal prudery and make it dumb.[35]

For, as the self-proclaimed guardians of morals should know, it is only when man goes down where the vital forces flow, harmonizing the body with the spirit, that he can avoid the misfortune of living in a personal hell where the body contains the spirit.

---

[34] Ibid., 118.
[35] Ibid., 121.

II. THE GOLDEN MEAN

Most of the poems contained in *Daedalus and Other Poems* are pure lyrics. Whereas *La Via* is concerned with the spiritual journey, *Daedalus and Other Poems* projects man's temporal sojourn.

Reminiscences. The lead poem is a poem of reminiscences. Demetillo speaks through the person of Daedalus, a mythical figure. Out of heavy stone and airy towers, Daedalus tells his story.

> Out of heavy stones, the airy towers!
> The artisans shaped the rock to fit my plans
> Traced on papyrus by deftness of my hands.
> The highways lengthened, purpose paved on plains
> And bronzed obeyed the coaxing of my skill.[36]

Man subdues the land but is suppressed when the flesh rules over the spirit.

> So we subdued the land, and having tamed
> The recalcitrant rocks to field the park,
> The land subdued us in the palaces
> The women primped and aromatic airs
> Defiled about them, as their lovers did.[37]

Progress brings laxity, and laxity, gross excess. Priests prophesy dazzling destinies and are believed, for such is the power of faith. Sages reason the mysteries in the halls of the academe. Seers and poets are deified, their monuments cramming the public parks. Matrons whet strange appetites. Progress is the rage. Nobody listens to the censors who see the destruction of civilization in the complete overhauling of the old customs. But hubris, that ever-faithful nemesis of mortals who want to be gods, swiftly slips in to demand an accounting.

---

[36] Ricaredo Demetillo, *Daedalus and Other Poems* (n.p.: 1961) All poems considered in this section are to be found in the same work.
[37] Ibid.

> So hubris overflowed through door and gate,
> Straight to the lowing pastures where one sought
> A bull-necked vehemence to glut her need.
> The island rocked, shocked by that gross excess.
> How should we dream the rot was cored in us?[38]

Hubris takes its toll. All the evils of a civilization materialize into a mythological monster, which in its coarseness, shapes man's perversity. Whose fault is it, the maidens'? the mothers'? the infants'? Corruption spreads as the weeds choke the vines, the palace walls grow drab, and the sewage spills onto the street. Within warehouses, furs feed the insatiable moths. Men imprisoned in themselves take to drink and dream of conquests. The death of civilization is certain: invasions and natural calamities compete with the people's extravaganza; the police themselves connive with mountebanks and thieves; the navies sent to war sink or skulk home in defeat. And yet, hubris hardens the heart of man. When experts are consulted regarding the rumor that the treasury is empty, they pronounce everything in order, and the demagogues have their day convincing everybody that nothing is wrong. Most of those concerned fail to see that they are destroying a civilization they have built. Daedalus, rather than witness chaos, flees to the golden mean.

> Rather than witness chaos, I prepared
> With cunning contrivance, the fabulous wings,
> Trusting alone to unswerving discipline
> To soar between the heaving sea and sky
> That narrow space where marvel is a flight.[39]

Discipline, humility, and moderation are required in this flight from the excesses of a civilization: neither too high nor too low—the level flight is best within the proper confine, between the earth and the sky. But in the proud, fierce daze of light, Icarus forgets the golden mean. He reverts to the excesses of the people he has left behind and suffers the avenging hands of hubris.

---

[38] Ibid.
[39] Ibid., 4.

> I warned against the crumpling up of pride
> But Icarus gyred upward to the sun.
> My nerves quailed as I watched that giddy flight.
> And when he fell, my old eyes were a sea
> In which he plunged forever out of sight.[40]

Thus dies Icarus, the symbol of a civilization wiped out by its overconfidence.

Civilization decays, and one grows old, burdened by memories. The myth repeats: visionaries are always scoffed at any age, in whatever clime.

> An old man now, burdened by memories,
> I dwell with savages who spurn my gifts
> And scoff to hear me talk of visionary shapes:
> Calm filaments of stone that shoulder skies.
> When will another Cnossus rear her spires?[41]

PART OF THE WHOLE. In this temporal sojourn, man is a part of the whole civilization. He survives, but not apart from his fellowmen. Man is a social animal, and he cannot run away from this reality.

To the poet, to walk at dawn is to think of fellow poets:

> This dawn I think of poets as I walk:
> Of Li Po in whose eyes the river entered
> When he, drunk with rice wine, decided
> To clasp the moonlight in the river sallows.
>
> And there was one put varve to wonder in exile:
> Tung Po who wrote calligraphy
> On silken parchments where the thews bulge out
> Bold as the wrist that shaped his magic.
>
> Who but Buson could, in the jewelled hokku,
> Transmute this dewdrop of a world
> That, granted is a dewdrop merely,
> Yet fascinates the mind of any poet.

---

[40] Ibid.

[41] Ibid.

> One thought of absence as she woke or slept,
> Feeling the wideness of the widowed bed,
> And emptiness of arms when death has hunted
> Brave hunters of dragonflies from winged meadows.
>
> And I who am the merest walking dot
> Beneath the sky from which cool silence drops,
> Have known exile and passion, delusion and yearning
> And known the sad shift beneath my feet.[42]

Like his predecessors, he has also known exile and passion, delusions and yearning, and the sand shifting beneath his feet. His being a mere dot beneath the sky does not exclude him from the vast procession of humanity, and he is so much a part of the whole.

"Eternity is not alone of time but feeling deeply, thinking much," when human sufferings try the spirit.

> What if I'm a speck in this great sweep?
> Of wombless time and limitless space?
> And what if grief has shaken down my days
> And that I may not wake from death-bound sleep?
> I'm still content that in my brief, brief time
> I've felt myself a part of one vast whole
> And known swift wonder swirl within my soul
> At seeing change in weather and in clime.
> I still rejoice that beauty's magic rhyme
> Can wile my spirit with its lyric flow.
> And from emotions and high thoughts I know
> Eternity is not alone of time
> But feeling deeply, thinking much, though pain
> Should bruise against the spirit's window pane.[43]

To be part of eternity, one has to be a part of "one vast whole." Demetillo is platonic in his concept of human thought. To him, the human mind is the reflection of the Divine. The source of every human thought, from

---

[42] "This Dawn I Think of Poets as I Walk," 9.
[43] "Sonnet," 11.

which the spirit draws life, is the limitless mind of God. The human mind participates in the activity of this one great thought which, in Christian philosophy, is God. By this, even a newborn infant is not a *tamquam tabula rasa*, since its mind already contains a portion of that one great thought stirring into activity as the child grows. Ultimately, all thoughts merge with the one great thought when creatures return to their Creator, as tributary streams do into the open sea. That is why human life, through the spirit, will not end.

> That which is part of us yet not of us,
> The oceaned source of every human thought,
> From which the living spirit draws, to which
> Our pilgrimage will at the last return,
> As mist in form of rain must run to sea—
> Will end not, though the flesh will putrefy
> And bones should moulder into lime and dust
> To brother the insensible clay. That which
> We do not see or touch but often calls
> To awesome surges of the mind, responding
> To its insistent knock, must, by its nature, be
> Like soul, yet as the likeness of the water-drop
> To that limitless ocean, the merging of the streams.[44]

In a way, Demetillo has Christianized Plato's concept of the immortality of the spirit.

The poet is one with the Pasig River, the orioles, the tethered carabaos, the herons, the kites, the oysters, and the herders—with all things in motion. He contemplates being one with April in branches where even clouds are caught, birds frolic, flowers dangle into fruit, and warm winds cross life. He is part of this series of movements, this concept of growth. He must build in inanimate objects, such as a piece of stone, the little miracles of delicate white boughs, fragile blossoms, filaments, and bars that stud the sea of life and link the islands to the continent. In the midst of it all, the poet is most aware that he is part of the whole, aligning his senses with the First Cause by the golden mean.[45]

---

[44] "Platonic Thought," 17.
[45] *Daedalus and Others Poems*, passim.

AWARENESS OF THE PRESENT. Awareness of the present is one of the virtues of the poet. Experiences pile up, some mystical, others mundane. "But he who swims with skill and courage tames/The waves. With firm but gentle strokes, he glides./The very waves will hold him up."[46]

This constant awareness of the present, this continuous search for meanings in the banal, enables the poet to maintain his composure without departing from the golden mean. Life is a classroom where one can learn, even from a dying penitent.

> The dying penitent, before his priest,
> Recites a rosary of venial sins,
> So heaven's ledger may credit in his name
> Repentance, and judgment to be lessened or dispensed.
>
> Fear-prompted, he unrolls his petty soul
> Till absolution rewards his provident thrift.
> Then he lies back on his complacent pillow
> And waits for death for there is nothing left.[47]

To be deeply religious, one has to be deeply aware of one's spiritual exercises. Otherwise, one will be just paying lip-service like

> The nameless women in whose faces linger
> The gloom of worry blue-black as their week,
> Blink at the glares that from rose-windows leak,
> Then fumble for their beads with cramped splayed fingers
> Laid by the memory of drab apartment
> Or lean-to in an alley where the stinks bloom.
> God offers each a sacramental Comb
> To straighten venial snarls in their department.
> Caught in the hypnosis of orisons,
> They soon forget the husbands on the booze,
> The wayward children and the garbage ooze.
> The Culpa shudders roofward with their groans.
>
> The paternoster is a need-forged chain
> Which, with Ave, links a fabulous hope

---

[46] "The Swimmer," 45.
[47] "The Dying Penitent," 46.

> That all the poor inherit. Still they grope
> The grovel, while brokers father on sly gain
>
> To buy expensive women, slick as cars,
> Or fly to Europe for a change of air,
> And be the proud butt of the envious stare
> Leaving no least trauma of the dent of scars.[48]

Religion guides its adherents toward the ultimate perfection, achievable only in the next life. But lack of religious awareness breeds indifference. People waste their lives doing things other than preparing for their spiritual future. Idlers browse pornographic paperbacks in sidewalk stalls; itchy minors drool sex in pursuit of hot perversity; balding and fatuous bachelors ogle the models in *Femme Spree*.

> What if the hungry and the poor
> Ride jeepneys of anxiety?
> Brisk is the business of the movies
> And cheap is phenobarbital.
> Let's leave all worries to the novice.
> You and I will not back the wall
> And moralizing is a bore.[49]

Without awareness, a concern can be fatal. Even solicitude can lead to slander. Prying eyes and tattling tongues can ruin a reputation, primarily a woman's character. Worse, they alienate man from others, creating a situation where self-interest nullifies clarity, and going with the herd makes for convenience.

> I am no Christ who'd stoop upon the dust
> While those who have accused her, shamed, would go.
> So, like a coward, too, I would turn my head
> And cannot meet the look of those slant eyes.[50]

Awareness of the present enables the poet to describe a lovely rite between a boy and his mother who recognizes every night upon his return home.

---

[48] "Women in the Church," 47.
[49] "Manila Sidewalks," 52
[50] "A Certain Woman," 54.

The awareness includes a world—Hinaktakan Beach, where the seagulls fly, spraying it with their flapping wings; Doris at Irvington, who sulks the song of locusts shrivels in the bare damped park. Furthermore, awareness of the present makes him write to a little girl with a promise to pluck a star or two to fashion a coronet for her. It makes him count the casualty list during World War II, draw a hero's portrait, and think of God on Christmas 1943. Eleven years after the first flight of an airplane, the poet is still aware that hate consumes the days of man and embeds the mind with shrapnels of mistrust and blight. Life, the poet is aware, is a continuous warfare. The safest way to live is to stay in the middle ground without being caught in the crossfire.[51]

Because life is warfare, a part of the poet is born on some battlefield. And yet, the Voice, which calls the countless stars by name, speaks his mind as conscience vigilant. Self confronts self. Between the nadir of hell and the apex of heaven, man wrestles with God. By denying God, has the poet been victorious?

> Laughing triumphant, I
> Hold my sides but heard my cry
> Fade in the wide
> And empty plain where we
> Had fought most valiantly.
> I knelt, felt the cold
> Side of One so bold;
> Then clasping that gashed side
> I cried, I cried, I cried![52]

---

[51] *Daedalus and Other Poems, passim.*
[52] "Tragic Victory," 80.

III. ANNALS OF THE FOREBEARS

BARTER IN PANAY. This book is a landmark in Philippine Literature in English because it is the first literary epic of the country in English.[53] As the author promises in his foreword, *Barter in Panay* is the first book of an epic trilogy that revolves around the life of Datu Sumakwel, the legendary first law-giver of Panay. But the second book turns out more than a decade later, not an epic poem, but a verse-play titled *The Heart of Emptiness Is Black*. *Barter in Panay*'s political orientation is no longer our concern here.

FLIGHT FROM TYRANNY. The epic narrates the so-called establishment of Bornean settlement in the Visayas, a "historical fact" at the time Demetillo writes the foreword to his epic, although contemporary Philippine historians now dismiss it as a folklore. Flight from the tyrant Makatunaw has compelled this Bornean people to come to Panay.

> Full ten years now is notched on our tree of life
> Since at Siruagan's Creek we anchored. Hope
> Had keeled our hulls that in this spume-fenced land
> Freedom would germinate like seeds we'd brought
> Far from Brunei, where Makatunaw grasped
> A despot's adocine and a murderer' sword.
> Rather than pour more blood on a gore-soaked soil,
> We fled the coasts of tamping tyranny.[54]

These fugitives are honorable men. Led by their nobles, they came with their wives and children in search of liberty.

---

[53] According to poet Federico Licsi Espino Jr., "Demetillo is also the first Filipino poet to write an epic in English–*Barter in Panay*, published in 1961 and immediately hailed as a masterpiece though contemporary critical thinking no longer carries that exuberance." ("Poets New and Otherwise," *Archipelago*, vol. III, no. 25 [1976], 31).

[54] Ricaredo Demetillo, *Barter in Panay* (Quezon: University of the Philippines, 1961), 1. Although Demetillo claims in his foreword that he has based his materials on history, he warns his reader beforehand that his is a literary epic. As such, he is free to change some names and places to suit his purposes.

> We rigged the wide sails and manned oars to find
> New seed-beds for the seeds of liberty.
> Ten datus sailed together with their wives
> And with them kindred maharlika braves,
> Faithful retainers both in war and peace,
> And many slaves to plow the virgin earth—
> All held by Datu Puti, minister
> Held high in councils of the government.
>
> He, in the throne-room of the tyrant, dared
> To number and impugn the bloody crimes
> Of Makatunaw, while that tyrant squirmed
> Or gnashed his wrath between dark-beteled teeth.
> While in the dark cave of his mind, he wrought
> The details of the cursed act which would strip
> His wife and child, which made him poor indeed.[55]

A flight from tyranny is a flight from wickedness. If we look at it from a religious point of view, the epic is an allegory of good and evil, the latter persecuting the former. The ten datus escape from the tyrant because their moral judgment no longer coincides with his. Datu Puti's speech to the tyrant, which costs him his wife and his child and his comfortable position in the regime, is an indictment of sin, a reiteration of the theme of the golden mean.

> "Reduce the number of your concubines.
> They drain gold, morrow of your monarchy.
> Live in frugality, that noble state
> Between luxuriousness and penury.
> Restore the seized estates and lift the tax
> And goods will fill the stalls and give you gold;
> And if you throne stern virtue, underlings
> Will walk the straight path, which is probity.
>
> "Spurn probity and evils plague the state,
> Like fleas on doddering dogs, and it is prey
> To other kingdoms better disciplined;
> For nothing worse invites invitation than
> Internal weakness caused by tyranny,

---

[55] Ibid.

> And when dissensions from within has gnawed
> The posts that prop the state, invaders need
> But little force to wreck the edifice."[56]

Sin, therefore, to Demetillo, weakens man's morale. Freedom is detachment from moral corruption, and progress is the fruit of a virtuous life. Once a ruler is enslaved by sin, he destroys freedom and becomes a tyrant.

PROPHETIC VISION. The early Filipinos are always looking for signs from heaven. They always correlate their lives with the will of their *anitos*. The high priest is a discerner of symbols, the conjurer of visions: "'See where the fingers of the gods now write/With scrawl of herons on the pod of heaven./Veer for those peaks the swift course of our ships.'"[57]

Some are undecided about whether to push back or welcome the fugitives and turn to fortune tellers for answers. The graying Polpulan, the revered father of Chief Marikudo, appeals to the wise men and warriors of the tribe to heed the prophecy of the fortune tellers:

> "Listen to me. Before I took the throne
> As chief, a fortune teller told me this:
> 'You will not die until brown strangers come
> To barter gold for your patrimony.'
> I have long pondered on that horoscope,
> When young, I laughed at it, but now I'm old;
> And when my son came back and told us this,
> The prophecy came back convincing me."[58]

The prophecy comes true. Girum, one of those Aetas hostile to strangers, gets impassioned and lambastes the cowardice of the former chief. Polpulan, a believer in fortune tellers, suffers a stroke and dies on the spot. Immediate death is meted out to the skeptical. When Chief Marikudo

---

[56] Ibid., 12. This solution is very simplistic.
[57] Ibid., 2. Bang-gotbanwa (Banggot-banwa in *The Heart of Emptiness Is Black*) speaking.
[58] Ibid., 79. The use of the word "horoscope" here is obviously improper. Another flaw: Demetillo treats the Aetas, with their council meetings, as a well-organized community, which is not so.

realizes the tragic turn of events, he puts the responsibility on the gods: "'Oh, horrid hour that amity should crack!/In this, we are the losers, and the gain/Goes to the strangers. Gods have wrought this trick.'"⁵⁹

Rishi Lakshman, a hermit who has the gift of prophecy, discourses to Sumakwel on man's dependence on God: "All things are linked to God, links of a chain/As you are part of one whole, mighty tribe."⁶⁰ The discourse does not stop there. The hermit also implicates what kind of sons and daughters romp the island of Panay:

> But always they will find the human heart
> A land still unexplored and beckoning,
> For in that little space is hell and heaven,
> Wilder than galaxies that stud the skies
> In it are secrets waiting discoverers,
> And whose dark journeys there should be as brave
> As yours who seek to course uncharted seas.
> Your people will unfold such mysteries.⁶¹

RELIGION AND SUPERSTITION. In *Barter in Panay*, there is already a hint of Kapinangan's falling for Gurong-gurong, Sumakwel's cousin, and of Gurong-gurong's being smitten by his cousin's wife. Their love is consummated in *The Heart of Emptiness Is Black*.

---

⁵⁹ Ibid., 81.

⁶⁰ Ibid.

⁶¹ Ibid., 57. We are with A.G. Hufana when he writes: "...*Barter in Panay* is told by a peripheral member of the landing party of datus who later in the poem no longer speaks as the central intelligence of the story. Instead, the poet's own omniscience intrudes, especially in the prophesying parts, which consist of addresses to those who will be born of the datu race (recalling the publication of these addresses as separate poems to Villa, Arguilla, Nick Joaquin, *et al.* in little journals which Demetillo has now incorporated into this work). The point of view is dropped, as the excerpt here shows only too well. It is to be contended otherwise that the point of view is still there. [It won't be easy] to see its presence—the presence of the same speaker who sets out to tell the story but has long been relinquished before the end—in the man-and-wife intimacy depicted. It is evident that the poet's clairvoyance and stream of thought have preempted the poet of view." *Notes on Poetry* (Quezon City: University of the Philippines Press, 1973, 96-97). Cf. *Barter in Panay*, 132.

Gurong-gurong in *The Heart of Emptiness Is Black* is pictured as a radical in contrast to Sumakwel, who now represents authority and tradition after that successful bargain with the Aetas. Gurong-gurong, determined to carry on an affair with his cousin's wife, typifies defiance because his cousin is also the chief of the tribe. Kapinangan, the chief's wife, also has radical leanings. After interfering in a tribal matter that concerns the subjects and involves the tribal laws, she is rebuked by the chief:

> If you were not my wife, I'd be scandalized
> At your ideas which are dangerous.
> What do you wish: abolish our society?
> We who are powerful dictate the laws.
> This has been so in old times as in ours
> And still will be in the future years.[62]

Coming from the chief who has run away from the tyranny of Makatunaw, this assertion of power is almost like heresy. To which Kapinangan answers:

> Not in the future years. In that time, slaves
> Will walk like free-men, unafraid,
> No longer held down to their poverty,
> But like the rest, live on an equal plane;
> Or else, the streets will sput their hatred
> At those who force on them a life of want.
> Bugnay should live as high Mata-as does.[63]

Gurong-gurong is ironic in his attitude toward the gods. Upon learning that Sumakwel has gone to the hills with Baggot-banwa to appease the gods, he remarks: "My cousin never slackens in his task./I see he likes to play safe with the gods/By marshalling the deities for aid." The gods do not bother him, nor does he bother with them. He questions the applicability of the tribal laws and detests fellow oligarchs. To him, doubt is the first step to wisdom. The tribe is brutal, its rules fierce. No one is supposed

---

[62] Ricaredo Demetillo, *The Heart of Emptiness Is Black* (Quezon City: University of the Philippines Press, 1975), 10. The use of the word "Black" in the title is equivocal.
[63] Ibid., 10-11.

to ask questions but to obey the laws to the letter.[64] Sumakwel answers him, saying:

> Your views, my cousin, are very dangerous,
> Which, I advise, keep only to yourself,
> For they are rats to over-run the tribe
> And that, as chief, I will not tolerate.
> But though I think that you are heretic,
> I shall absolve you for I gave my pledge,
> Man is, by nature, full of lawlessness.'[65]

Sumakwel's belief that man is full of lawlessness by nature makes him a legalistic ruler. Enslaved by the laws of the tribe, he has made of his rule another form of tyranny just the same, though to a different degree.

High priest Banggot-banwa conspires with the State in perpetuating old-fashioned values, which reformers like Gurong-gurong have to go. He has chained, through superstition, the whole tribe to conventions. He preaches a religious fear, and God is a god of wrath who sends calamities to punish transgression. This is a very primitive way of confusing religion with superstition.

> As priest, I warn the plagues will worsen yet
> Unless we act with dispatch in this case,
> So all the angry gods will be placated.
> You as our leaders should find the secret cause
> And out it from the body of the state.
> Although those guilty be friends or relatives.[66]

Banggot-banwa is no better than the *babaylan* of the Aetas who, earlier, has warned Marikudo: "Blood defiles this place./Two ghosts flit over us and, unappeased,/They cast their evil spells. Beware that you/Because of all our sorrows."[67]

---

[64] Ibid., 17.
[65] Ibid., 40.
[66] Ibid., 48.
[67] *Barter in Panay*, 82.

> Farewell, Sumakwel. May your sleep be deep
> Un-haunted by your cousin and your wife
> Whose only crime is that they dared to love
> Scaling the very heights of ecstasy,
> Our minds free of the tweedle of the tribe.
> I deeply pity you, for history
> Will, in the future, know your real worth:
> A little man besides a brutal chief.[68]

In the final scene of *The Heart of Emptiness Is Black*, religion clashes with superstition: Kapinangan represents religion, and she wants the tribe to awaken to their senses long under the spell of the high priest. Banggot-banwa, on the other hand, represents superstition and resents the views of Kapinangan because, if the tribe accepted them, his *anitos* would lose their grip on the people.

> BANGGOT-BANWA:
> The woman is bewitched, bewitched by craft
> Shaped by Gurong-gurong's gibes and jokes!
> How can we let the land to be defiled
> By her who has no fear of all the gods,
> Whose anger flares at men's impieties?
> Her evil deed deserves a cruel death!
> Sir, if she lives, she will pollute our thoughts.
> Her beauty is a snare that leads to death!
>
> KAPINANGAN:
> You are fanatical in words and deeds.
> You have enthroned vile superstitions,
> Like the demons and the spirits you invoke
> Your kind destroys the common sense of men,
> A common sense more kindly than your creed![69]

Kapinangan's indictment of Banggot-banwa is an outright condemnation of a primitive belief that, to her mind, cannot be acceptable anymore. Her valedictory to Sumakwel is full of prophecies. Someday, when religion is purged of spirits and demons, history will know the chief's real worth.

---

[68] *The Heart of Emptiness Is Black*, 70.
[69] Ibid., 72.

In this chapter, we dealt with the works of Ricaredo Demetillo, which have one theme in common: the journey of the human spirit. We have found it in his books *La Via: A Spiritual Journey*, *Daedalus and Other Poems*, and *Barter in Panay*. We have also deemed it practical to touch on his verse drama, *The Heart of Emptiness Is Black*.

La Via underscores the fact that every age needs to have its spiritual journey written by its particular poets to maintain the psychic health of the epoch. *La Via* is premised on the presupposition that man's spiritual and creative fullness can be achieved only through the proper exercise of their psycho-physical functions, especially sexual. Guilts, anxieties, and even madness result from an over-rigid denial of such functions. The institutional Church is accused of being obsolete and an obstruction instead of a guide in man's spiritual quest. One cannot expect much from the Church's guidance. God's saving grace and love elevate man and help him reach his original innocence. In his spiritual journey, Demetillo's message is clear: one must not neglect or despise the way of the flesh.

Daedalus and Other Poems concerns itself with a physical journey, a journey of the here and now, the rise and fall of civilizations. Even as man journeys here and now, he must practice moderation or the Greek's golden mean. The spirit must not be laid aside or left behind in man's temporal journey toward fulfillment. Life on earth is a preparation for the next life.

Barter in Panay speaks about the checkered history of the early Filipino people. They were fugitives from the tyranny of moral corruption, and theirs was an attempt to establish a reign of peace and justice. But even then, superstition beclouded their original purpose, as pointed out in *The Heart of Emptiness Is Black*. Man is enslaved by it until he becomes another tyrant. Might becomes right.

From the preceding books, we can deduce the following conclusions: 1) a spiritual journey is always a flight from wrong values—a hypocritical religion as in *La Via*, a crumbling civilization as in *Daedalus and Other Poems*, moral corruption as in *Barter in Panay*, superstition as in T*he Heart of Emptiness Is Black*; 2) to commence one's spiritual journey, one has to reconcile first the body with the spirit; 3) to arrive at Eden, one has to arrive at original innocence through the mystery of love.

CHAPTER III

MASKS AND SIGNATURE

Being religious and aware, Ricaredo Demetillo speaks of the total condition of man in society. Demetillo's poetry, the late top Philippine diplomat and author Carlos P. Romulo observes, "is not evasive but consistently concerned with the human condition, sensitive to the nuances of the critics, either in the individual psyche or in the social order."[1]

I. THE WAY OF ART

Masks and Signature evokes and celebrates the artists. In a real sense, it marks the tradition of the intellect and the imagination, which is absolutely necessary for the creative life. This tradition, the poet insists, is derived not only from the local but also from European, American, and other sources. The book is meditational, central to grace in the artistic and religious sense.

ARTISTS DEFINED. "I should define the term 'artists,'" Demetillo writes in an essay, "not in the narrow sense that would include only the visual group but also the artists who engage in the creation of poems, short stories, novels, dramas, music, architecture, and even performing arts, for each of

---

[1] Critical comment, *Masks and Signature* (Quezon City: University of the Philippines Press, 1968), outside back cover. All poems considered in this section are to be found in the same work.

these groups is faced with new problems and new challenges unique to this particular period in our history."²

The artist in our society wears many masks. He is part clown, part fool, perhaps a martyr to love. His face outwears seasons: It would be too much to claim that he is politic, for he can also be an *arbolario*, the betel-nut-chewing primitive medicine man with the juice of the bitter leaves spewing through his teeth. He is a healer, too, though part mountebank.

> Now let me tell you what I am indeed:
> Part clown, admitted; fool, admitted too;
> For in these days, I wear my motley wear
> And dunce-cap flaunts above my mop of hair.
> Perhaps, a martyr—only to love; all else
> May seem unclear—dust, certainly, and wind.
> I tread on bombast as on a sagged trapeze,
> Then kick the poles that all the tight-wires fall,
> Bow to my audience, which is just myself.
> Disclaimers? Yes. But who would not disclaim
> Against all other faces of more papier-mâché ?
> My face at least will wear out seasons; I
> Shall not say for the rest of you; but then,
> I'm not politic, though that's a claim too much.
> Lord Haw-Haw wriggles up my comic sleeve;
> Also an Arbolario, for the primitive,
> With betel-nut, is spewing through my teeth:
> Part mountebank but then a healer too.³

To create, the artist starts with nothingness, "that awful emptiness which glares before the eyes, where talent gasps and dies." On that blank sheet of nothingness, "one must gaze until it spurts a blaze of knowing miracle." The artist is another Adam who starts to call creation "each by name that is as pure as flame." If he is a poet, the artist forges the poem word by word "until it cuts strict like a sword." Truth is the hardcore of art. What is false or uncouth must be rejected.⁴

---

² Ricaredo Demetillo, "Filipino Artists in the Early 1970s," *Solidarity* (December 1973), 41.
³ "An Artist," 1.
⁴ "Ars Poetica," 2.

Art is a lonely pursuit. The artist must explore deep in the human heart to bear and subdue the dark to let harmony rule the blood—the artist orders to purify. Art demands stern discipline, for grace is the privilege of an artist. The artist is Columbus at sea before he discovers the firm continent. Since the artist is involved in a struggle with "dark human fate," he may be crushed before the conflict between creation and reality shall have been resolved. Hence, the artist's solution to his problem in his art is, in a way, a resolution of the problem of life and death. Inspiration, that "dark Sphinx," bares the truth to the few; it speaks only once and may not speak again. Therefore, the artist must be all the more receptive to inspiration and pour wholly of his love to gain communion. Art is communication in the first place. "The poem bridge *I* to *you*/Over which hovers God's bright dove." The epitaph of the martyrs applies to the artists: "Who loses life gains it anew." The nights and days of an artist are lonely: "At times, one crawls a bone-bruised pace/At times, one chews a meatless bone." The way of art is truly "a strange saw to the frugal flocks."[5]

The artist's genius is a vast void that no creation can fill its need. When a genius dies, he leaves behind him the treasures mined by his labors. There are few or none who will weep for a genius at his death.

Now the question is: would other geniuses resume the strife after his death?

> Sir, what is genius but an emptiness
> So vast no creation can quite fill
> The awful void of its needs; hence, leaves
> No peace but fumes at its own littleness
> And what is fame but smoke that may not still
> Ambition, terrible as hell that heaves?
> The genius drags his desert and his thirst
> And in his sleep dreams of the aching blank
> Which he must fill, a demiurge in a heat,
> That all the sterile wilderness should burst
> To bloom, with no form of impotent or lank,
> But full of vigor, regored by his feat.

---

[5] "The Way of Art," 3-4.

There is no rest, no faith, no law except his own.
His face, implacable to dominate,
Strains on supreme and cruelest distress.
He is his own hell where the devils spawn
But which he grapples in both love and hate
To ease—or so he hopes—fierce loneliness.

There is a lust for conquest in his eyes
And on the pavements, he treads, a conqueror
And thus walks, few to love him as few would love
A Genghis Khan beneath the envious skies.
What unheard continent would he now explore?
What guardian knot to cut? What secrets to prove?

This is a monomaniac of desire
Searching the secret of both life and death,
Of being and non-being with no arms
Save mind and will, inflexible as fire,
Fed by bituminous fierceness, till the myth
Is forged, insidious in its dark, fierce charms.

Yet when the task is done, the aches remain.
He execrates the heavens that the world,
So ill-made, should be ill-disposed to him
Whose titan labors are the world's vast gain.
Would men ignore the passions he has hurled
Against their faces and would time be dim?

This is the terror chasing him in sleep
And so, irascible, preys on his mind;
And each audacity diminishes his life.
Spent at the last with none or few to weep,
He leaves the treasures which his labors mined.
Would other geniuses resume the strife?[6]

A few years after the publication of *Masks and Signature,* Demetillo would tell this writer: "I would like to think that my works are a constant striving to rediscover man in his inmost significance. What are we but constant pain and a remorseless stumbling in the labyrinths of the world around us, so hard, so materialistic, so concerned with the surface aspects of the

---

[6] "Genius," 5-6.

sensate life, unless we are aware of this inner vibrancy?[7] One sometimes pays for being an artist; when a crisis exceeds one's capacity to suffer, a nervous breakdown occurs, and this becomes the artist's calvary."[8]

The artist is Proteus. He must capture the sounds of the sea, for they are the mirrors of man's nature. When still, each tone of sadness, each ecstasy, each undulating synergy of the sea, is arrested by the Nereid's skill in choosing a house; this lover of the sea sees to it that his house faces seaward. Below the artist, as Proteus is always death, the mystery as cold as seaweed near a quay. The sea is a cycle of metamorphoses: the vast image of eternity, the green cradle where life is born, and the vast waters where all return. The corruption of one is the generation of another. The artist, therefore, should not be mourned his death. For all we know, he will rise again. The nourishment is bread.[9]

The artist as navigator always starts from one familiar part, gathering and learning from experience. When he dares the unknown, he shares the pride of great discoverers at sea.

> One always starts from one familiar port:
> The sea coast graphed upon a map,
> The currents inked upon a chart.
> All is in their place; the helmsman most alert;
> The weather jaunty as the sailor's cap.
> It is when land is out of sight that he
> Who pilots should bestir himself,
> Lest there be storm or mutiny.
> It has been known before, unhappily,

---

[7] Letter of Ricaredo Demetillo to Gilbert Luis R. Centina III, OSA, dated August 12, 1972, Quezon City.

[8] "The most important thing is that you are gaining new and deeper experiences and that you are improving your draft to project these experiences. You're the type who profits from all possible experiences, including the unpleasant ones. The latter are necessary as the happier ones to add dimensions to your thoughts. I hope you will be equal to the crises that happen in your life. Some of us writers pay such crises by having nervous breakdowns. Pray that you won't undergo that calvary." (Letter of Ricaredo Demetillo to Gilbert Luis R. Centina III, OSA, dated April 5, 1972, Quezon City).

[9] "The Artist as Proteus," 7-8.

> That ships go grounded on a hidden shelf.
> The journey could be just the usual trip,
> Something that we know needs to be done
> Without much fan-fare and no slip.
> Or it may be a journey on a ship,
> Say, to explore the coast of what's unknown.
> Since it is special, then we trust that he
> Who navigates shares in the pride
> Of great discoverers at sea
> Daring all hazards that the mystery
> Be bared and commerce ply on the far tide.[10]

Sometimes the artist succumbs to the Circean lore, but the live column of light that emanates from his art enables him to transcend all bonds. He is everyman: a man on holiday contemplating the play of light and shade; a passenger boarding a bus for suburbia where his wife reheats the leftover soup from lunch to serve for supper; a naturalist feeling the sun as a friend that showers him with gifts; a realist; a surrealist; a Hamlet in his Elsinore.[11]

To Demetillo, the test of true literary greatness is commensurate with the amount or degree of illumination that a writer can focus on the totality of the human experience. "That is why Shakespeare is judged by us [as] the greatest of writers because he has illuminated as many facets of our human situation as is possible for a mortal to do. That is also...why Dostoevsky is such a great novelist, possibly the greatest the world has ever known, not because he has advanced political revolution in Russia. What is the greatness of El Greco or Michaelangelo except that they...have stretched the dimension of understanding?"[12]

Eschewing art for art's sake and art as socio-political propaganda, the consummate artist can well say:

> Abolish all geographies
> Save one.

---

[10] "Navigator," 21.

[11] *Masks and Signature, passim.*

[12] Ricaredo Demetillo, "José Garcia Villa vs. Salvador P. Lopez," *The Authentic Voice of Poetry* (Quezon City: University of the Philippines Press, 1962), 308.

> Abolish all these boundaries
> Defined by zone:
> Arctic, torrid or temperate.
> Abolish all:
> At any rate,
> The old topographies,
> Both big and small.
> Abolish all.[13]

The works of some artists are a constant striving to rediscover man in his inmost insignificance. But, of course, there is so much beauty even on the surface of life, so much that it achingly finds a response in all of us. Some artists do nothing else but record this surface and still find a certain kind of validity. A great artist oscillates between these two opposite poles.[14]

PRAISE OF UNSTABLE MEN. The second section of *Masks and Signature* is about the "witnesses" of art whom Demetillo praises for being unstable men. Instability must be understood as loneliness, and art is a lonely pursuit. The artist must be prepared to be lonely in practicing his craft because he is actually a miner of the most prized jewels of the mind.

> I sing the praise of all unstable men
> Whose fertile lack of balance fructifies
> The formal gardens they retrieve from swamps
> And girdle warmly with incandescent lamps
> So that the marsh beneath inhospitable skies
> Twines now with clustering grapes, a nourishing plain.
> Consider how the jewels we most prize
> Are mined from darkness by those light-dazed men
> And by those divers to the depth that yawns
> Beneath us when we loiter in the dawns.
> Those found our cure who fevered in the brain
> And mapped the light though darkness mired their eyes.[15]

---

[13] "Abolish All Geographies Save One," 13.
[14] Letter of Ricaredo Demetillo to Gilbert Luis R. Centina III, OSA, dated August 12, 1973, Quezon City. Demetillo here is talking about Quasimodo. Beauty is always internal, and oscillating between these opposite poles may lead one to mediocrity.
[15] "Praise of Unstable Men," 58. The use of "incandescent lamps" here is inappropriate.

Aliens and self-exiles in their labor, the artists make restlessness a starting point of their genius. They become a package of contradictions. Although they are dispossessed, they can still bring to humankind the rare possessions of their restless breasts. From their spend-thrift hearts, these prodigals filch treasures to men's pampered feet when they themselves are being deprived of a place to lay their heads. Only after death, when light triumphs over all, do they get the laurels about their brow.

> They find homes for our spirits who themselves
> Find only unfeeling stones to lay their heads
> And build our heaven though their hells gape wide
> And darts and bullets hiss life from their side.
> Out of frail dreams, they build a durable bridge
> To what is possible—our finest selves.
>
> Poor in all else save in their love of the art,
> They win our freedom by their servitude
> To that which is a drug to their addict hearts.
> Do they not live on pittance from the marts
> And struggle on a cramp of solitude
> From which they flee—to arms of bore or tart?
>
> Buffoon or mad knave, mountebank or prince,
> They lie in death, a lawful prey to worms,
> Who in their lives most lawless often move.
> Only dark beauty's order do they love
> And for her stern sake wreck all previous forms
> To find that form to order hordes of sense.
> Fame which, alive, they seldom get but crave,
> Laurels about their brow when they are dead.
> Deft chisels monument their haunted face
> While critics graph the lineaments of grace.
> All share their miracles of song like bread.
> The light once more triumphs over the grave.[16]

The witnesses of art are followers of light. There is Van Gogh, in whose brain the sun is a bright god, and he becomes so enamored with the light that everything turns into total darkness in his soul.

---

[16] Ibid., 59.

> Out of the dark holes which his loneliness
> Defined with tatters, he saw the Son of Man
> And, devotee to that god, took his faith
> Among cramped minors dawn a shark-gaunt path.
> That faith dragged heavy as a cross to stun
> This staggering man to stark Gethsemane.[17]

"Dying is hard, but living harder still." The usual saying turns out to be Van Gogh's epitaph. Unloved by women because to them he was unattractive, and he flees from a decalogued town to be alone with his Muse. On each green leaf, he paints his desires; in each phallused cypress, he sublimates his ecstasy. Considered mad, he cannot sell his paintings. Forsaken by the bright sun god, the devotee of light shoots himself, flaming upward "beautiful and rare."[18]

Gauguin's desire is to strip himself and be "simple as Magdalenes in their cave." He mourns progress as a sterile trap and entombs the city streets with drab grey walls in his paintings. Choked by the dust of Paris, eyes blinded by the city's glare, he takes to flight, "shipped on a dare," and casts his anchor in a bold light.

> Enchanted by the islands of his dreams,
> The canvases become pure poetry,
> Simple and sumptuous in their loveliness,
> Hinting no boredom and no pettiness.
> Love flowed in brown, blue, yellow sensuously
> And sunlight rippled on the dappled streams.[19]

Modigliani takes drugs to erase the bleared, bleak daubings of "ignominy." Obsessed by the problem of evil, Baudelaire, with his hashish pipe, proves that marvels of dark nourishment can grow out of the Gehenna's excrement. Mallarmé has a vague yearning in his aesthetic soul.[20]

---

[17] "Vincent Van Gogh," 60.
[18] Ibid., 61.
[19] "Gauguin," 63.
[20] *Masks and Signature*, passim.

Blake is a theologian who sees a universe in a grain of sand, a holy innocent who writes on the fellowship of all creatures, and a man of faith who thinks life is a series of miracles. This poet is always aware of man's beatitudes as well as frustrations:

>   Blake met God early and the universe
>   Became a witness to His majesty,
>   And in his mind a skyline arched where He
>   Was sun to ostracize Urizen's curse.
>   Urizen was the power to darken us
>   And made prim prudence prune the body's tree.
>   Imagination felt the infamy
>   Which wilted buds and blossoms—odious loss.
>   Jesus's religion was not morality
>   Else Socrates were saviour of the world.
>   Jesus, Divinest Body, is forever curled
>   In love, about the bodies of you and me.
>   Only when man fulfills his needs for love,
>   Not flagellated to a skeleton,
>   Can man sing alleluiahs to God's throne
>   And let the poem's praise to rise above.
>   Praise is the ritual of all art
>   And study, prayer which lifts the Host.
>   The dilettante is sodden anti-Christ
>   Or Judas who betrays marvel in the heart.
>   He saw a universe in a grain of sand
>   And lambs danced with the tiger in a glade.
>   All miracle is trembling on a grassy blade.
>   And marvel lies in the hollow of a hand.
>   So seeing wonder, how he grieved to know
>   That churches shadowed Albion like a shroud,
>   The children blasted by a lustful bawd,
>   While men's frustrations shaped the shapes of woe.[21]

The poem discloses that: 1) to serve God is to renounce Satan; 2) religion is distinct from morality; 3) Jesus fulfills man's need for love; 4) only when love is adequately fulfilled, not through the flagellation of the body, but good works, can man sing praises to his Creator; 5) praise is the ritual of all art; 6) the artist must believe in God.

---

[21] "Blake," 90.

To Tagore, all song is praise, a sacrament sung with the most divine art in solitude. The flame of art is present in Szu Kung Tu, who counsels kings; in Tu Fu, who, indifferent to glitter and to show, sings out of a simple heart; in Lin Po, who sings of friends whose hands he held in greeting or else pressed to say goodbye; in Lady Murasaki who cannot falsify the human heart just to please her noble audience; in Kuryosai to whom design is all and mystery its ends; in Hokusai Ghwashiki who, true to his art, insists on the integrity of the line.[22]

Hieronymus Bosch's world disintegrates like a fruit. He sees hell wherever he turns his eyes, "Not like the conflagration cracking gloom/But where fierce avarice, concupiscence/And lusts unbridled whet their appetite." He makes all classes of men wallow in the Stygian sty,/And only Christ retains the human form,/With young Veronica rapt in a trance/Who sees not maniac leers of lust and spite." If hell gapes as gulf, however, in the art of Bosch, heaven also gleams. The human and divine, held in contempt, "drags a cross weighed by all the bestial ilk, whose legion visage is a caricature of truth." Bosch paints man, not as man seems outside but as man shorn of all masks that culture makes. "A beast that takes delight in cruelty/And murders with his looks as with his lies."[23]

Novelist-dramatist-poet Cervantes loves the world but sees it dark. Betrayed by his illusions, this Iberian genius has learned the profound lore of the wise. In his Catholic Spain, where religion has become a mockery in spite of the people's strong faith, Cervantes confronts life with a satire "sly and pat." To Cervantes, man is the mark of all derisions; the world as it is crucifies the heart of man.[24]

Painters, too, are critics of their time. Botticelli depicts the actual condition of his time. Sanzio, the Lord of Order, paints Satan pinned down by Saint Michael but curiously makes the eyes of the imps sad. Goya's reaction to his country, "a cauldron boiling with hate," is a cruel kind of art that sets men free. Delacroix wrestles angels in the night, "The massive body strained to keep its hold,/His figures lifted from massed humanity/Flowing past him, each with a lark, lost face."[25]

---

[22] *Masks and Signature*, passim.

[23] "Hieronymus Bosch," 102-3.

[24] "Cervantes," 104-5.

[25] *Masks and Signature*, passim.

Blind artists must not be overlooked. They also enrich themselves through their craft.

> Homer sang from the clear dark of his eyes
> Of heroes striving with the gods for fame
> Bought by their young lives on the plains of Troy;
> And blind Beethoven, did he not deploy
> Genius against dark Fate to flash his name,
> A first class sun among the galaxies?
>
> But old Teiresias with unerring hand
> Pointed at the darkness which would blast the eyes
> Of Oedipus and dangle his spouse.
> Likewise, did Milton, is a groping house,
> Sing of high idyll in bright Paradise
> Where tempting apples turned to gritty sand.[26]

The artists are as diverse as their art. Daumier, having known the grind of poverty as well, limns man with sympathy, realizing that at least man has his dignity. Vermeer's base for art is the gross seduction of the flesh. Art for Picasso is exuberance, not excess. Picasso's art is true communion born of humility. It accepts the gifts of genius from the past, which celebrate the heart and cast the odyssey of man in durable form. Rembrandt's art plumbs the mystery of living with its wonders, joys, and woes. Homais draws the perils of adultery and warns of dangers brought about by marital infidelity to the family. Stendhal knows the emptiness of power. Hawthorne's art is a whirlpool of belief and unbelief. Exorcist or genius Melville dramatizes the terrors of killing by making the seven oceans one colossal stage. Wallace Stevens is a go-between for the marriage of truth with reality. W. H. Auden considers the poem a higher kind of play; the poet is an artificer of words. St. John-Perse sees beauty as nothing but a gift to a man who dies[27]

In society, artists assume the roles of psychologists, moralists, and philosophers. Freud is an artist, too, in his own way. "Freud showed all our common tragedy/And we would not know hope but for his cue." He has

---

[26] "The Blind Ones," 116. Actually, Beethoven was deaf, not blind. Inaccuracies of this kind are not uncommon in Demetillo's poetry.

[27] *Masks and Signature, passim.*

been part of the air man breathes, the shaper of man's liberty. Proust is a giant larva in his flat, weaving the present and the past into myth, where time is forever brilliant. *Fear* is the scepter that annuls Kafka's heart. God, to Dostoevsky, is not dead: He is only there in the frozen dungeon of man's heart. Disorders in communal life stream straight from disordered men. Between the Scylla of the puritan and the Charybdis of the instincts, André Gide sails with this battle cry: "Be yourself." To ape proves tyrannous hypocrisy. The immoralist, wittingly or unwittingly, is also a moralist.[28]

Saint Augustine is one of the mountains that define one's consciousness, a terrific psychologist and a guilt-love-driven man. For this wisest of the holy and holiest of the wise, the human heart is restless until it rests in God. Pascal believes that "the heart has its reasons which reason knows nothing of." Man is reconciled in Christ. Kierkegaard, the philosopher of life's contraries, considers life a sacrifice. Through his works, he has demonstrated that "on a tilting ship, storm-threatened, there is faith none may destroy."[29]

FILIPINO ARTISTS. Sixteen Filipino artists are given signal recognition, some of them for the first time, in the section titled "Witnesses" in *Masks and Signature*. What is the image of man as projected by Philippine art and literature? Perhaps, more accurately, one should not speak of an image, but rather of the images that Philippine art and literature present, for, indeed, with the diverse talents at work in creating aspects of life in our midst, the impression tends to be multi-faceted. Coming from various social levels, the artists naturally tend to project those aspects of the reality most appealing to them.[30]

The Filipino in José Rizal is a reformer, a dreamer of true religion.

> Rebellion blazed on his brow like a sun
> And having knowledge felt his people's dark

---

[28] *Masks and Signature, passim*. In his poem on Sigmund Freud, Demetillo's concept of tragedy seems to run counter to the classic notion that tragedy brings about purgation.
[29] *Masks and Signature, passim*.
[30] Ricaredo Demetillo, "Image of Man in Contemporary Art & Literature," *Humanities* (no. 4), 8.

And knew how cheerless were their days and night(s)
Who feared to move lest pitfalls fracture bone
And lest each shadow pounce, a devil, stark
And terrifying to their caving sight.

Born to a father too proud to bow the knee
And to a mother who had taught him love,
He read experience like large alphabets
That spelled the odious word of TYRANNY.
He heard the whispers at the cooking stove,
At table and the cockpits near the belts.

The books that nourished him told of a God
Who, in His love, made Himself man like us
So we might know redemption and be free
To walk as equal children through His blood.
But *frailes* wrought inequality, abuse;
And *frailes* engineered such infamy.
He knew the Christ was sold and was betrayed
By those who commerced on His holy name.
The poor worked to the bare bones so to pay
But all the country was a land of shame
And brigands waylaid victims by the way.
The priest who took the vow of poverty
Moved earth and heaven to compass a land
Cleared by a peasant from the wilderness
Or charged a fortune from the tenant's fee.
The masses groaned beneath the cassocked hand
And stored the venom of their bitterness.[31]

Rizal is gentle, trained to heal, but stern of purpose, unafraid. He nurtures dreams until they become adamant. He is Prometheus undaunted by any god; he is the moth that circles the light; he is the artist concerned with the humanity of his race.

---

[31] "Rizal," 71-72. "At table and the cockpits near the bets" is an awkward construction. "The *fraile*'s shadows..." (*sic*). It was Dominican friars who were involved in an agrarian dispute with the parents of Rizal.

> The Spaniards called his people *chongos*; he
> Would demonstrate that they were human, too,
> Carving the contours of proud poetry
> And using knowledge that the thought be free
> To follow flight of eagles in the blue
> Or build a home sacred to liberty.[32]

Before martyrdom, the artist is an expatriate. He eats his heart out in loneliness on foreign shores. He wanders and sees for himself the manners and the mores of other people enjoying the boon of freedom. Exile hastens his dreams to grow, and with the thoughts ever winging back to his faraway land, he speaks of the plight of his people in his novels. He pours the bitter truth out so that "tyranny be laughed out of these strands."

> The pages bristled and accused each shame,
> Blot on religion and the cause of man:
> The good men driven to a life of crime,
> The causes of their fall all writ in flames
> The child made ignorant by pious ban;
> And goatish lusts ringing the pious chime.
>
> But such impudence, such effrontery
> Could not remain unchallenged; all his foes
> Become a band of Furies laughing at this one.
> But in his land, his gospel set man free.
> The acid laughter mocked each priestly ruse.
> Respect for Spanish power was also gone.
>
> They shot him on a field, but not before
> The ardor of his love had flamed to freedom's dawn.
> His was a life complete—what more was there
> Than his name be written in the lore
> Of all truth-seekers in this free-man's zone
> And that his honor blazon all the air?[33]

Writing about the nineteenth-century painter Juan Luna, Demetillo sees Luna's use of the canvas to denote the cause of tyranny and oppres-

---

[32] Ibid., 72. The Spaniards called the natives *"indios,"* not *"chongos."*
[33] Ibid., 73.

sion. Luna was the first internationally recognized Philippine artist for his award-winning paintings in Europe. While in Spain, he and other Filipino patriots like Rizal formed the Propaganda Movement, which advocated for political reforms in the Philippines. Beneath the cautery of his skill, Luna diagrams the cancerous growth which has sapped a colony in paintings that are bold protests.

> Twitted that he was born to a stunted race,
> He towered to the sky and brandished grace
> That all who saw him were amazed. His fame
> Offset the dark night of our shame.
>
> He carved not with the sword but with the brush
> Which in his fingers prophesied the crush
> Of empires flung across the galleoned seas.
> Each stroke hacked down harsh tyrannies.
>
> He saw the terror and the violence, and he
> Depicted sorrow, too, and infamy.
> Corpses are dragged across a blood-soaked sky
> Youths, brutalized by what they hear and see,
> Laugh at the latest perfidy.
>
> This is an accusation. Dispossessed
> Himself, the genius raises his bold protest.
> A king admires his skill but fails to see
> The cancerous growth beneath the cautery.
>
> Heedless, the throne shook and an empire cracked—
> A mighty edifice by earthquake rocked.
> The race, despised, regained its liberty.
> The crouching victims stood up—free.[34]

Twentieth-century Filipino writers, depending on their psyche and experience, have messages to the contemporary man: Carlos Bulosan, who dies in extreme poverty in the United States, wishes to warn his compatriots "of danger, tense and curt" that a Filipino or any foreigner from the Third World may meet in the land of the greenback. "America was cold,

---

[34] "Luna," 74.

cruel, indifferent/And women, too expensive such as he." Manuel Arguilla, a peasant's son with the peasant's gift, writes about peasants' simple but happy life. To Arguilla, it is only in the cities that the eyes grow dull. There is no brotherhood in the city between cap and lowercase; men are classified according to their wealth and stature.

Novelist N.V.M. Gonzalez shines a light on the lives of people in the *kaingin* who refuse to be dehumanized by poverty and earn respect from others through their strict work ethic. They carved a place for themselves under the sun through honest manual labor. In this harsh setting, man finds "true identity." Nick Joaquin, perhaps the Philippines' most well-known writer, conjures a golden time—the glorious Intramuros of long ago. Poet José Garcia Villa rebels against his elders by horrifying them with his sonnets "dressed up in common and pampered polka dots." After toppling down the dull elders, the narcissistic iconoclast mimics God with Christ, his brother. "The Christ Himself bows from a proud bright skull/To greet this haughty Cavalier and Priest,/Before they stroll and esoteric songs/Drip like honey from their mystic tongues."[35]

The twentieth-century Filipino painters paint the image of man and his environment with a contemporary touch: Anita Magasaysay-Ho takes in capaciously the ordinary folk: vendors and busybodies, giggling girls and women bantering raucously, maids doing the laundry. Magsaysay-Ho, in her works, tries to capture the elementary things in life: the sweep of headgear, the shape of a leaf-like eye, the brownness of a face, the light that glows on limpid moments, the form that sings "before the heat of living makes it dry." Constancio Bernardo makes hunting an art. José Joya Jr. is a traveler, an exile from his native land. Wherever he goes, he sees a sign of vegetation, even in the aridest environment, including the desert. "The pristine purity of light is there,/As vital forms dance on the canvases." Vicente Manansala goes abroad to perfect artistry, only to return home and discover that all the art he could know is in his backyard. He paints peddlers, roosters, carabaos, trees, churchyards, plaster saints, Christ jeered at by the crowd, poor people with scanty victuals at a meal, and children by a low stone wall, the broken and the maimed. "It is not mere

---

[35] *Masks and Signature, passim.* The poem on Nick Joaquin is originally titled "Born in an Age of Lead"; that on José Garcia Villa, "Cavalier and Priest."

paint he brushes but his love,/The piety for common things he knows/It is compassion from his fingers flows." Poetry and grace move in his paintings. Fernando Zóbel, a scion of an aristocratic family, still opens his thoughts to the poet even when he depicts an era long gone when proud *hidalgos* held sway and continents kneeled before the *conquistadores*. To make himself contemporary, though, he paints dons sitting behind an office desk, "But still the feet must pace the restless floors/And hands obey the firm will which commands." There is elegance in the lines of Arturo Luz' paintings and melody in the swerves of their contour. Spare like a poem, his clinical art moves to almost pure geometry. Robert Chavet Rodríguez is a calm voyager to eternity. His paintings of a row of houses at nightfall are a dance of dark and light. Romeo Tabuena, seemingly unaffected by his New York stint, manages to capture the Filipino soul by putting into canvas native houses, carabaos, tropic sun and moon, and a star tipping a pole near the nipa caves.[36]

The artist as a painter is summarily given recognition in the poem on Hernando Ocampo, the "artist" to whom the volume of *Masks and Signature* is dedicated.

> Flee from the arid city where each street
> In bier where men, though living, are immured
> And eyes are semaphores to signal their distress.
> Theft boredom is a willing bloom and spoored
> Heart is trampled by the hunter's bestial feet.
>
> Only in love's green country may the thought
> Find roots to greenly clasped maternal earth.
> There rocks are changed to verdure and the vine
> Becomes the nourishment in us, like wine
> Poured on a crystal beaker brimming mirth;
> And marvel is the smelt of melonous fruit.
>
> The sap's bright arrow, shut from quiver-bole
> Becomes the light that dazzles as it streams.
> All, all is luminous and marvel-clear
> To zenith of the mind's pure atmosphere.

---

[36] *Masks and Signature, passim.*

> As if the birds have choired upon our dreams
> And herons parachuted banks of soul.
>
> The artist standing in corridors of eyes
> Beholds the bright horizon, splendor-dazed,
> Through aperture where swirls the shadow's gloom,
> Then paints awe's balance with a nerve of ice.
> He captures splendor by which he is graze,
> The poem's fields all tremulous with bloom.[37]

Considering that Hernando Ocampo was an erstwhile poet before dedicating himself to painting, this poem is Demetillo's declaration that the hierarchies of art are interrelated. Whatever medium an artist may use, the artist's two-fold aim is to serve and delight.

GOD AND THE ARTISTS. Demetillo's archetypal symbol of artistic activity is almost always the search, a journey that involves incredible difficulties. The labyrinth is part of this journey, too. As often as not, one is lost trying to escape the dreadful mystification of that labyrinthine passage. "Divine Poems of Eliezer," the final poem in *Masks and Signature*, is rich in archetypal symbols.

> I've wandered in every latitude and zone.
> I, like Odysseus, knew the Cyclops's cave
> Where I was no-man with sharp stratagem;
> And I was Theseus chained to Pluto's stone
> Before I was released out of my gnawing grave;
> And I was Oedipus, blind by Jocasta's hem.
>
> I was Orestes when he plunged the knife
> That killed his mother and her lover; then
> Was strung by Furies when that deed was done
> To stumble through the brambles till his life
> Was spared by highest wisdom and a glen
> Became a garden where he sat a throne.
>
> In Palestine, I had the brand of Cain
> And was the prodigal that fed with swine,
> Driven by scorpion-gullets low as the dung

---

[37] "Hernando Ocampo," 89.

> And I was Pilate, too, that feared the din,
> Then washed my hands of Christ and went to dine.
> I spat at Him and trolled a drunken song.
>
> And I was Lazarus, cold in his tomb,
> All swathed in grave sheets, till that Voice was heard
> Which crocked the seal of Death and woke my eyes
> To see One shattering all that horrid gloom;
> And I was Peter shamed by the growing bird
> Who rushed our penitent beneath the skies.[38]

The different personae, mythological and biblical, represent the different masks that the artist can assume. On closer inspection, one notes that the personages chosen from the Bible are, in one way or another, connected with salvation history. On the other hand, the figures lifted from Greek mythology are either defiant to the gods or victims of the god's machinations.

The artists participate in god's divine plan. Herein lies their religious significance. Only god can give rest to the artistic mind.

> God is my place of rest. I've wandered far
> To seek the certainty the world can't give.
> My pride, all shattered, knows humility;
> And love, which is the bread He shares with me,
> I share with others that they too may live
> And know His glory in each sun and star.[39]

Aside from proclaiming the glory of God, the artist also sings his praises.

> This is not building but a song of praise
> Or rather song made visible for all to see
> That only as the Lord walks with us men
> To share our labor, may this joyless den,
> Which is the earth, know too that harmony
> That angels chorus to the Lord of grace.[40]

---

[38] "Divine Poems of Eliezer," 172. Theseus was never "chained to Pluto's stone."
[39] Ibid., 173. Cf. Saint Augustine's *Confessions*: "You have made us for yourself, Oh, Lord, and our hearts are restless until they rest in you."
[40] Ibid.

Redeemed by Christ, the artist is one with him in creating order and dispensing joy.

> Yet this is a paradox that we who are
> Bought by the Lord all walk in liberty,
> No longer slave to passions that destroy
> But master and inheritor of joy,
> Dispensing joy, too, we sense and see
> Grace ordering the heart, sun, moon and star.[41]

Acknowledging the power of the Creator, the artist magnifies God in his life and art:

> The stones, subject to Time, will fall apart
> And lose communion in the earth and grass.
> But those who know God will seek other stones
> And teach them speech to sing love's fervid tones.
> They will not build on dogmas which too pass
> But magnify Him with their lives and art.[42]

God is limitless. He embraces all creatures and causes the sun to shine and rain to fall on everyone—the interchange between the artist and his fellowmen in the systole and diastole of life. The work of art manifests Eternal Beauty. God, in the world of tangibles, is completed in the artist.

> How else is God completed but in me?
> I also bind and heal the broken grief
> Writing songs leavened with joy and grace.[43]

Thus, in his kinship with fellow artists, Demetillo has concluded that God, the Alpha, and Omega of creation, is the Way of all arts.

---

[41] Ibid., 174.
[42] Ibid.
[43] Ibid., 175.

II. THE SCARE-CROW CHRIST

Demetillo's *The Scare-Crow Christ* contains socially conscious poems. And this volume also includes poems written in Hiligaynon, Demetillo's native idiom. The verses in *The Scare-Crow Christ* deal with the poor and most exploited. Christ is the highest level of being men can attain, but the ordinary man is a scarecrow in society.

MAN DIMINISHED. The title poem starts with mourning for a man unfulfilled because diminished, whose life is a living death.

> I mourn man, man diminished, unfulfilled,
> Whose shadow drags the darkness of his night
> Across the endless dreariness of days,
> Where no oasis greens the sand-choked waste.
> I mourn for man, my brother crucified.[44]

This "brother crucified" does not have a specific name. Despite his miseries in life, he can be anybody who is meek and mild like Christ, never losing hope, forever making a better future that may never be his.

> Though doom ticks through the clammy cells of blood,
> Hope pendulums the marrow of each nerve.
> I know his hungers scoop the lake for snails,
> His guts Gehenna with their appetite
> Prowling to thieve the larders for his lock.
>
> In room where locusts crunch the dog-eared crop,
> Despair bisecting thought in fields of blight;
> In forms where claw-like fingers wear to shreds
> And huts precarious sag down to the grave,
> This man still sidles in a search for light.[45]

---

[44] *The Scare-Crow Christ* (Quezon City: University of the Philippines Press, 1973), 1. Hyphen *sic*. All poems considered in this section are to be found in the same work. We purposely exclude "The American Voyage" because it does not serve our purpose.

[45] Ibid.

The brother becomes a neighbor in need who is refused admission as often as he knocks at the door to seek help.

> Is he not neighbor to my creaking bed
> When sleep weighs at the eyelids like a rock?
> His cries croak down the echoes of my heart
> Though often I would spurn his rattled knock.
> Is he not neighbor to my creaking bed?[46]

Conscience disturbed by this scarecrow image of Christ, the poet appeals to his reader:

> And you, my reader in this cramp of words,
> Are you not party to his hang-dog gait?
> You tear his blankets to a chill of shreds,
> Scratching your fat feasts from his patient plate?
> Are you not Judas to his scare-crow Christ?[47]

Those who can afford more in life are party to this poor man's fate. Society has betrayed this man who is poor because others are rich.

From the universal man, the poet descends to the specific: an old man tottering on a city street.

> An old man totters on an urban street.
> His short, frayed at the collar and the sleeves,
> Balloons, as if he were a scarecrow with a stick;
> But sparrows do not fright at his approach,
> Except that I, half-pitying, half-repelled,
> Look at him closely as he stumbles past.
> I hope that in twenty years, a fate unkind
> Would not cause me to totter as he does
> A chance remote, or so I like to think.
> "What does he live for?" one might ask:
> A bit of rice shared by indifference?
> A snatch of sleep beneath an underpass?

---

[46] Ibid.
[47] Ibid.

A busted pair of shoes so he could walk
The pot-holed streets where traffic tremors past?
Is not his sleep just a short reprieve
From grimy waking up to another sleep:
Belly, a tyrant that forces him to beg,
A palm stretched out to catch a coin dropped?

But maybe waking up is something sweet
So he could feel the warmth, the air's cool touch,
And see up in the sky a bit of cloud,
Radiant as silk and also marvelous,
This beggar totters past, his shadow, black
On pavement pitiless as summer heat.
My rapid transit, bisected by my thoughts,
Leads me among the vendors where shouts
All advertise the goods but not the God I seek.

A stone's throw and a church looms near the road,
Its shadows darkening the lane I pass.
The newsboys hawk day's calamities
And shames that nothing can excuse or gloss.
The brown-veiled women grovel in the dark
Or burn a candle for lack-luster saints,
That float on clouds of incenses
Above the sorrows of the multitude,
I turn. Two beggars whine, their hands outstretched.[48]

    The poem is a subject worth a brief analysis. In the first stanza, an older man tottering past him catches the poet's attention. His first reaction is one of half-pity and half-repulsion. He tries to look at himself and hopes that he will not be like this old, helpless man in twenty years. From superficial observations, the poet goes to the heart of the matter in the second stanza. He starts worrying about the older man's livelihood and survival. The image of the older man haunts him. Then, in the third stanza, the poet's thoughts of the older man are interpreted by his impressions of the surroundings. The city is noisy; everybody is preoccupied with his affairs. In the fourth stanza, the irony materializes: newsboys peddling the calamities of the day, pious women groveling in the dark, or burning candles for "lackluster saints." The church looms on the road, but the saints seem far

---

[48] "An Old Man Totters on an Urban Street," 2-3.

away or else irrelevant. Society is ruthless. There is not only one older man tottering around in rags; when the poet turns around, two beggars whine, their hands outstretched. There is no mention of anyone giving alms.

The whole poem can be interpreted thus: some people worry about the lot of the poor, but they do not do something concrete about it. This is the real irony of the whole poem.

Indifference diminishes the ordinary man and leaves him unfulfilled. A youth may go out to fight a war he never planned and dies in the hands of enemies he never created, and still, life goes on as usual. Between wars, "the rude god grins upon the mocking page," yet those not affected sleep late and wake, "eager enough to rise and shine" and make their mark. While the mansions of the rich are lighted, poverty erects its huts to one side, "protests in the pallid dusk." Those who should care to leave the country, those who should not go insane, and those who cannot stomach life anymore end their "threadbare life" by committing suicide.[49]

Claw and fang rule in the wilderness of the metropolis. Man who, to Demetillo, is the glory of the universe[50] becomes a beast of burden, a victim of exploitation by his fellow humans. Brotherhood is trampled upon in this battleground of survival where beggars, assassins, opportunists, profiteers, unscrupulous executives—all finished products of a cruel society that has divided its denizens into rich and poor, exploiter and exploited, elite and outcast—elbow one another out.

> The boulevards are thickets where the beggars thrive
> And where assassins lurk to gun down their prey.
> The peddlers shout to wake the very dead:
> There, claw and fang dictate their decalogue.
>
> The finned automobiles slide by on grease,
> And over them, the furious neon bleeds.
> The secular religion of age
> Shrills from each jukebox in the crowded kicks.
> Profit is what these denizens pursue.

---

[49] *The Scare-Crow Christ*, passim.
[50] "The Glory of the Universe," 18.

> Up in their business suites, executives,
> The high priests of the new religion, talk:
> They also have the power to bind or loose.
>
> But in the groceries and market stalls,
> The anxious wives peel peso bills and frown
> To see prices rise beyond their reach:
> They know that hunger is a hollow pit.
> So, through the day and well into the night,
> The crowds mill at the sidewalks, till the nerves
> Slacken the headlong pace in a short reprieve.
> The beggars huddle in the underpass.[51]

Tired and alien in the city, his coat unable to keep out the cold, the poor man finds respite only in death.[52]

Religion, which teaches the dignity of man, has become a simple act, something like insurance that one must have—those who do not care to buy a policy never bother about the least of their brethren. Good Friday is spent like any other day, and calvary is shrugged off with a beer bottle.

> Why should my mind hark back to One
> Who hangs upon the tree?
> I call for beer to quench my thirst
> And shrug off calvary.[53]

The gaping difference between the haves and the have-nots is spelled out by the following poem, which narrates an incident that occurs one typical Easter morning:

> It's Easter morning and the moist air
> Vibrates with sounds of crispy life.
> In kitchen rise the fragrant smells
> That stir our manly appetite;
> But on the kerb, one scavenger
> Sorts out the trash that suffocates the air.
> My wife has come, a sunrise worshiper.

---

[51] "The Metropolis," 46.
[52] "Elegy for Narciso," 45.
[53] "Holy Friday in the City," 19.

> She talks about the jolly Easter eggs
> Hidden by palms and bushes on the lawn
> That children sought to appropriate.
> The scavenger curses to be heard,
> Enough to wake the dead.
> She says the pastor's sermon was a "beaut,"
> So hopeful and so pat.
> The ladies treated all to dutch.
> The food was plenteous, all were satisfied.
> The rugged fellow with the skulking gait
> Has found a tattered piece of bread.[54]

Are the poor who still have the strength to work as laborers any better than the beggars or scavengers? To Demetillo, they are pathetic figures just the same. They resemble God only because, like him, they labor all day. Unlike God, however, their hands have never known beatitude, and their hands are too coarse to feel or give much love. Theirs is to hammer and smash to earn their daily diet of rice and fish.

> Spread out upon a meager board, they move
> Like talons to tear the flesh of fish.
> Cereal is masticated by the mouth,
> Viand demolished by the furious teeth.
> Whoever said that eating is a rite?
> I am appalled by what I goggle at.
> Fingers can gesture, sure and elegant.
> Here all is brutish, angular and rough.
>
> They never knew in full their heritage
> To carve the air with gravity and grace,
> They fumble at the shreds that were a shirt:
> Their hands, too coarse to feel or give much love.
>
> Dürer drew hands that labored at trade
> And etched them in the attitude of prayer,
> Each vein and muscle alive to intercede
> A God that loves to labor through the days,

---

[54] "A Tattered Piece of Bread," 28.

> These hands have never known beatitude—
> They clench into a fist to hammer and to smash.[55]

As beggars or laborers, the very poor are always diminished and unfulfilled in society. He is a scarecrow, having no alternative but to be crucified to a life of hardship.

MAN STRUGGLING. The fourteen Hiligaynon poems included in *The Scare-Crow Christ* are Demetillo's first attempt at Hiligaynon poetry to be included in a book. As the careful reader will notice, these poems are still sophomoric. Due to his having lived for so long in the Philippines' sprawling Metro Manila capital region, specifically within the University of the Philippines campus in Diliman, Quezon City, Demetillo is not totally at home with the nuances of the dialect. His grammar is defective; his syntax unsure of itself. The spelling he adopts is inconsistent and confusing, not the one used by veteran Hiligaynon writers such as Ramon L. Muzones, Conrado J. Norada, and Magdalena G. Jalandoni.

However, it is not for us to discuss the mechanics of Demetillo's poetry in Hiligaynon. Instead, our task here is to analyze the content, which is the saving grace of his poems.

The first poem is about the sun, whom the poet calls a friend. The smiling sun wakes him up, urging him to get up because there is so much work to be done.

> Gatamwa ang adlaw sa akon nga kuarto
> Ang iya nawong naga kadlaw.
> "Hoy, magbangon ka na, *hijo*!
> Madamu ang imo hilikuton."[56]

The sun's invitation to work is well taken. The sun itself exemplifies the joyful worker. It is a good and kind friend: it ripens the fruits of the trees.

---

[55] "Laborer's Hands," 51.

[56] "The sun is peeping at my room,/Its face is smiling,/'Hey, sonny, get up!/You have lots of things to do.'" ("Amigong Adlaw"/"Friend, the Sun," 80.) Translation of Hiligaynon poems is ours.

When it does not shine, heaven is sad; when it does, everybody is happy, and the children are filled with laughter.[57]

Having identified himself with the everyday joys of the ordinary person, the poet, speaking through a hedonist, invites the poor people to dance and sing. Once a man dies, he will sleep forever. Songs and dances will cease like the bubbling *estero*; the greedy earth will swallow up children, adolescents, and the old. Man must love now; tomorrow, the chords of youth may be broken. "Sa lulubngan, Inday, wala sang pagsayaw;/Kag ang aton lawas lapakan sang karbaw."[58]

The poet teaches the ordinary man how to appreciate art. Even if the statue is limbless or headless, it nevertheless manifests freedom because it is a product of the free genius of the artist. The figure smiles gloriously; its beauty brings happiness. The sculptor who carved the statue has freedom in his thoughts; his dream is imprinted on the beautiful statue, the vision of what is beautiful in the human body.[59]

The very poor do not know what joy is. How can they perceive the beauty around them when their eyes are always downcast? The working class has no occasion to look at the blazing sun, and joy is strangled within their breasts.

> Ano ang pagkakita nila sang katahuman
> Nga ang mga mata yara sa ila talapakan,
> Wala nagatamud sa gabadlak nga langit.
> Ang kalipay nakuga sa ila nga dughan.[60]

In crowded towns, people have to snatch their food from the streets. How, then, can they dream of the future?

---

[57] Ibid.

[58] "In the grave, dear lady, there is no more dancing;/And our body will be stepped upon by the carabao." ("Isang Hedonista"/"A Hedonist," 81.) Cf. Andrew Marvell's "To His Coy Mistress": "The grave's a fine and private place,/But more, I think, do there embrace."

[59] "Estatua Griega," 82.

[60] "How can they perceive beauty/When their eyes are downcast,/Unstaring at the bright sky./Joy is strangled within their breasts." ("Kalipay Nakuga sa Ila nga Dughan"/"Joy Is Strangled Within Their Breasts," 83.)

> Ila gin-agaw ang ila pagkaon
> Sa higad sang dalan sa gutok nga banwa.
> Makahuna-huna bala sang dalamguhanon
> Ining kailo man nga mga timawa?

At home, the child has a fever and needs medication. The parents are bitter about it; they have no money to remedy the situation.

> Sa ila balay may hilanat ang bata,
> Kinahanglan bulong agud mag-ayo sia.
> Mapait ang ila binabana-bana;
> Wala sang puhunan nga magihit nila.[61]

The roof leaks due to the rain. Tomorrow there will be no rice to cook, and the problem is too big for them. Where can they steal money?

> Ang ulan gatulo sa mga atup nila,
> Buwas wala sing bugas nga ila tigangon.
> Ang libug mabug-at nga ila dalal-on.
> Diin and pilak nga ila kawaton?[62]

Strait is the road for the poor. Poverty has driven them to snatch and stab. They are no longer afraid to be killed or imprisoned; fear and shame have vanished altogether.

> Gani ang mga dalan gagutok sa ila
> Maabtik magagaw, bisan pa magbunu.
> Nadula ang hadluk o kon kabalaka
> Nga sila mapatay o kon mabilang-go.[63]

How is the life of an ordinary employee? Does it have any meaning at all? The typical schedule of an ordinary citizen, according to Demetillo, is as

---

[61] "At home the baby has fever,/Medicines are needed for its cure./Their thoughts are bitter;/They have no savings which they can use." (Ibid.)

[62] "The rain leaks through their roof,/Tomorrow there will be no more rice to cook./The problem they have to carry is heavy./Where is the money that they can steal?" (Ibid.)

[63] "And so the road is crowded for them:/Swift snatchers, they go to the extent of stabbing./They have no more fear or concern/They die or go to prison." (Ibid.)

follows: wake up and yawn, wash face, take breakfast and coffee, hop on a jeepney to go to work, kowtow to the boss, put in time from nine to five, board another jeepney to go home, take supper, listen to the radio, and be in bed by nine-thirty in the evening. This humdrum existence seldom ever changes for the common man or woman.

> Magmata kita kag magpangnguy-ab;
> Manibin, mamahaw, maginum sang kape;
> Magsakay sa jeepni nha pa opisina;
> Magduko sa "boss" kon magsugo sing iya;
> Magobra walang takna tubtub a las sinco;
> Magsakay sa jeepni kay mapauli na;
> Manihapon kag mamati sang radio
> Kag tumulog kon mag a las nueve-y-media.
> Buwas, amo gihapon ang aton baton himoon,
> Wala sing lain-lain sa bilog nga semana.[64]

With this schedule, will there be time for such luxuries in life as swimming on a beach, cultivating an orchard, writing a poem, attending a concert, visiting Baguio or Pagsanjan, carving a statue, witnessing an Ati-atihan festival, hunting a deer, hearing the *Song of Roland*, reading the counsels of Buddha?[65]

The scavengers are already at work early in the morning, dumpster diving to salvage whatever they can. Demetillo likens them to lice infesting the head of the town, the disgrace of society. They are human beings yet devoid of ambition, and Christ is unknown to their illiterate hearts.

> Sila amo and kuto sa ulo sang banwa:
> Sila and aton kahuy-anan.

---

[64] "We wake up and yawn;/Wash our faces, take breakfast, drink coffee;/Board a jeepney, office-bound./Bow to the boss when he orders whatever pleases him;/Work for eight hours until five o'clock;/Board the jeep because it is time to go home;/Take supper and listen to the radio/And sleep when it is nine-thirty./Tomorrow, we will be doing the same things,/There is no variation whatsoever for the whole week," ("Ano: Ang Kabuhi Mo May Kahulugan Bala?"/"What: Does Your Life Have Any Meaning at All?", 84.)

[65] Ibid.

> Tan-awa sila sa ila pagduko-duko.
> Si Cristo wala sa ila nha dughan.[66]

Moved by love and compassion for his suffering brethren, the poet looks at his own family. Everybody is working hard except for an idle nephew who does nothing but hangs around with his *barkada* and eats and sleeps. He feels sorry for him. He also remembers his father, who had gone to Mindanao to join many homesteaders. Now he is a poet, while his father has long been dead. He asks forgiveness from the dead. His poems are a testament to his repentance because they are dedicated to the hardscrabble people like his father.[67]

Now a grandfather of a lovable child, the poet sings a lullaby to the grandson. Tomorrow, he sings, the pains that stalk and shadow life will begin when the child grows up. Meanwhile, the child must sleep freely.

> Magtulog ka sing mahilway, O hinigugma.
> Yari ang mha butkon gahamil-ay sa imo.
> Sa buwas nga damlog, kon ikaw na daku,
> Ang kasakit kag ang mha ho-ol madamo.[68]

Soon after, the sun will rise again, calling everybody back to work. The poor and most exploited, the scarecrow image of Christ in society is now prepared to take up his usual calvary. There is no sabbath for the scarecrow.

THE AUTHENTIC SELF. The poet notes around him the "tortured grimaces of laughter burnt to cinder like a toast." From the simple folk, the poet has learned to face the days ahead without pretense. He throws his mask and puts on his genuine self. It takes heroism to be authentic: "To look at one's friends with a steadfast gaze,/To shake a hand or share a laugh is bliss./To

---

[66] "They are the lice on the head of the town:/They are our ignominy./Look at them in their downcast state./Christ is not within their hearts." ("Basureros"/"Garbage Scavengers," 85.)

[67] *The Scare-Crow Christ*, passim.

[68] "Sleep freely, beloved one./Here are these arms to give rest./Tomorrow, when you are grown to youth,/There will be plenty of pains and cares." ("Dilambong sa Akon nga Apo"/"Poem for My Grandson," 89.)

look at enemies unflinchingly at their hate/Takes courage like an Ensor's or a Christ's/Ringed by sadistic leers or scowls of rage."[69]

This authenticity leads the poet to an awakening. Rebuked by his Muse for singing what has been sung in the past, for merely singing for the sake of singing, he becomes socially conscious.

> But my stern Muse rebuked my startled ears
> Sing of the dark declensions of the time:
> The fractured vision seen through scalding tears.
> But sing, sing in close harmony and rhyme.
> Sing of disasters that shutter at our door
> During these decades, idiot with our wars.
> Sing of love and faith struck down by knuckled power,
> And all the young men twisted like their scars.
>
> Sing of the fallen fences where the herds
> Stampede from meadows to the sheep ravines;
> Sing of the corpses strewn on the riddled yards
> And corpses spraddled beneath the blasted pines.
>
> Consider too the hate festering the air.
> Buds wizen on the boughs like all the fruits.
> The dead may dangle from the sodden stair,
> The neighbor's lawn trampled by brutal boots.
>
> As Hokusai saw Fiji's shoulders gleam
> Between the heaves of inundating waves,
> Find order in the wreckage of our time
> And meaning snatched from dark gorgonian caves.
>
> Absurd, perhaps, most gestures of the pen
> Yet you will shape dark Beauty there
> To stir the sense and mind of thoughtful men.
> The rest is silence. Poet, you must dare![70]

So the poet sings of an unknown woman, now dead, who had never known any honors in her life but hardships: dawn saw her labor in a stony field, earning a pittance to buy rice for her daily sustenance. He sings of

---

[69] "The Authentic Self," 17.
[70] "The Fractured Vision," 33.

a poet-monk who writes on the corruption of the Church without any fear. His prose is unadorned like a hammer, smashing down to shape the luminosities of truth: a bludgeon with gown and crucifix—that rare, bold thing, "a conscience that attacks." He sings of the possibility of his going insane by some freak of fate. He sings of the river of his youth, death, the old bastard, and the phobophobic man suffering from anxiety. He sings of the poor and most exploited, made in the image of God but forsaken in society.[71]

> I could have been one of the chosen twelve.
> I would have leaned upon the breast of love
> Or tried to weigh price-money in a bag.
> I might have heard the signal crow of guilt
> That burst the proud boast blanching in the night.
> I might have been one of the fickle crowd
> That cried their vivas, then spat in spite;
> For in myself spawn all the hates
> That torment flesh and blood before they cast
> The javelins at man's quivering side.[72]

We discussed the artist's role in society in this chapter, according to Demetillo. The artist wears different masks. Depending on his psyche, he writes about his age; he is, in fact, a witness of his generation. Art is a calvary. Only in God can the artist find rest because only God can still the restlessness of his spirit. Therefore, the artist is God's instrument in this world to proclaim, glorify, and sing his praises in the world of the tangibles. Through his life and art, the artist participates in God's completion.

Christ is the highest level of being a man can attain. In society, however, the ordinary man is a scarecrow. The artist feels an affinity for the poor, having known human suffering himself. The artist signifies the poor through his art. Demetillo has eschewed art for art's sake and art as propa-

---

[71] *The Scare-Crow Christ*, passim.
[72] "The Glory of the World Rode on an Ass," 31.

ganda. For him, the artist should deal with the totality of man in society. He can write about fellow artists who dabble in the spirit realm. Still, he can also write for and about the simple people, diminished and unfulfilled, the image of a scarecrow Christ. In this society of masks, Demetillo has affixed his signature to the totality of man. After all, God, whose image and likeness man is created, is the Way of all arts. An artist is a free man. This is a religious statement from an all-religious spirit.

RICAREDO DEMETILLO

The city and the thread of light
Update the barter in Panay,
Like Lazarus who celebrates
With gratitude and joy his resurrection.
Neighbors in want are the scarecrow Christ.
Exposed to no certain weather,
Shunned by religious bureaucrats
Crippled by the darkness of their hearts.
Your terrible sonnets, for just reasons,
Lash at the clericalism of cassocked jerks
Who preach the wrath of an angry god
And turn their churches into a marketplace.
Since sin is not central to your faith,
But the healing, forgiving love of God,
The autobiography of your troubled conscience
Brings you back to your father's home.

—Gilbert Luis R. Centina III
From *Triptych and Collected Poems* (New York: Centiramo Publishing, 2013)

CHAPTER IV

LAZARUS, TROUBADOUR

The Second Vatican Council has wrought changes in the Catholic Church, if not Christendom. The censorious *Index Librorum Prohibitorum* has been abolished, the word "*anathema sic*" has been deleted, and the previously sinister term "heretics" has been reworded to a more benign expression, "separated brethren." With the declaration of "Religious Freedom," Ecumenism has replaced the medieval Crusade as an appropriate measure in settling religious disputes. The message and meaning of the Ecumenical Council have been published under the title *The Documents of Vatican II* with notes and comments by Catholic, Protestant, and Orthodox authorities.[1]

Ricaredo Demetillo, who has been following developments in Christianity, is aware of these changes in the Church.[2] We must consider this in analyzing his published volumes of poetry, *The City and the Thread of Light and Lazarus, Troubadour*. The poems in these collections are poems of religious enlightenment. The poet, who used to be dissatisfied with the institutionalized Church, has found authenticity in the Church because of its effort to return to early Christianity in liturgy and worship. In finding goodness, truth, and beauty in the reforms initiated by the ecclesiastics, the poet has finally found himself.

---

[1] Walter M. Abbot, SJ, ed., *The Document of Vatican II* (New York: Guild Press, 1966).
[2] Interview with Ricaredo Demetillo.

I. THE CITY AND THE THREAD OF LIGHT

Manila, "that we half detest and half love," forms the background in the spiritual quest, both artistic and religious, that is evoked in *The City and the Thread of Light*. The names of places are familiar, but in the light of that search, they are somewhat transformed. "I like to think," Demetillo writes in his preface, "that the search evoked in these pages is a profoundly reverent one, a real celebration of the *Via Cristiana*.[3]

One noticeable thing in the City poems is the invocation to Israfel: "That flaming angel that often visits me/In solitude and my bleak despair/To bring me solace is bright Israfel./A marvel and sacred mystery." The invocation speaks about "Love that searches and that never dies," the love which, illumined "by the Son that warms my days...brought the chaliced Wine my spirit sips." The last stanza is a consecration: "Ah, Israfel, I consecrate my life/To that Love which is the Highest Good./I bow in reverence before your Face/That is my beacon to the stars above!"[4] This invocation indicates that the City poems are meant to unify the religious with the artistic.

THE CITY OF MAN. "Imprisoned by the rocks, the city looms," the first poem, "Lost," starts thus, in the circle of the damned. Here the city is the ideal one, the spiritual, and the man speaking is lost, or is temporarily so, in the city of man.

> Obtrusive volumes block the passages.
> No man or dog can tease the rabbit's run.
> All, all is strenuous and a man is lost,
> Except his scream that shatters night like glass.
> The skies are lonely for the vanished sun.[5]

---

[3] Ricardo Demetillo, *The City and the Thread of Light* (Quezon City: University of the Philippines Press, 1973), p.v. All poems considered in this section are to be found in the same work.

[4] "Poem to Israfel," vii.

[5] "Lost," 1.

One critic observes that the correlative here is as heavy in sounds as in their metaphoric expressiveness.[6] Of course, one's alignment makes all the difference.

The pitiless glare reveals the horror of the city of man. Dust cakes the sagging walls and leaves decay; drabness is equal to the mind's dark ebb. Crowds stream like maddened currents, timed by the clock. The throngs, pursued by loneliness, are the lost ones, tottering on the streets. The city cannot give them love or joy. The city of man is a transitory place where man is outlived by art.[7] However, the religious poet, aware that the city of man is a passage mortals have to descend to ascend to the Eternal City, celebrates half in hate and half in love.

> I celebrate this City half in hate and love.
> Whether I view it from a plane or from the streets,
> Part call-girl, part slattern that appalls me quite
> By what I see or hear or smell or read about.
> Yet, she is what it is, our kin of sorts,
> At whom we laugh, derisive, when she turns her back.
>
> This female sprawls in languor near the sea.
> Her garbage flies upon the foetid streets.
> Esteros suck the filth where multitudes spill their diet.
> The bloated chicken or a skinned cat or a dog,
> Their bodies rafts of squirming colonies.
> The sea reflects a wanton's made-up cheeks.
>
> She is as public as any prostitute.
> Her bosom has embraced all kinds of loves.
> The proud Castilians heaved upon her breasts.
> So have the Chinese all these centuries;
> So have the Yanks that tickled her with lust.
> The Japs, too, bedded her to the boom of bombs.

---

[6] Louella R. Centina, "The City and the Thread of Light," *The Philwomanian* (September 1974), 5.

[7] *The City and the Thread of Light*, passim.

So all these years, with blowzy confidence,
In spite of change lovers, she has lived,
Dressed in her finery and dowdy rage—
Not quite a lady for she walks the streets
And beds with common sailors, merchants, pimps and thieves.
Her laugh pursues her lovers as they make exit.

Yet, if she is a harridan and her house
Is over-run with rats and countless relatives,
She pays loud praise to all the talented
Who share the verisimilitudes of grace,
Though she does not wholly understand what it is about.
The costly merchandise impressed her, I think.

The Lady in the Palace by the stream, of late,
Has given her a face-lift for the tourist trade.
Yes, she is dressed in colors, bold and bright,
The puddled streets tabooed to those who wish to see
Only relics of checkered yesterday.
We hide the dirt in our own native way!

But she is colorful, "a real character,"
Who laughs defiance down the ribald streets.
The tradesmen blare out their advertisements
Luring the customers to buy not always shoddy goods.
We cannot get along without this City. So,
I celebrate the Female half in love and hate![8]

One gets elbowed by the crowds, pushed this way and that, in this city of man where everybody is in a hurry. Demetillo describes the crowd as "just fragments of arms and legs, the sweaty bodies runneled by the heat, cut to a half, a quarter of a third."[9] This is a picturesque way of saying that nobody is perfectly whole in this City, that everybody is striving for that something—call it happiness or fulfillment—unattainable for the present. Each has obligations to buy groceries, meet a date, engage in business, and seek solace in beer bottles.

---

[8] "I Celebrate This City," 4-5.
[9] "Elbowed by Crowds," 6.

It takes darkness to reveal light. Bare branches of *kalachuchi* in a Tondo patio, "burnt against the light, seem darkly organized and twist and imprecate a distant heaven." "Prince Valiant wields the mighty Dinging Sword in Quiapo Alley. Ermita is a tourist spot where art vies with casinos, occasional scandals, and *toro* shows. "Cunning is naked in the vendor's eyes" in Quinta Market. Fort Santiago is reduced to ruins made of "rain-dark stones that used to pillar colonial majesty." The ruins "bear up to the stresses of the century through flaking bit by bit like ancient bones." "How shall we justify the horrors of this age? Will bleak historians falsify the facts?" The cityscape is hideous in its ugliness; death is mannered in memorial parks.[10] The poet here and there picks familiar landmarks, retouches them, and presents a portrait of the city of man, personified in Manila. This city cannot satisfy its inhabitants because of its distractions. The Holy Grail may be found right in this city, but higher things are subordinated to the fulfillment of the littlest dreams.

> This City, labyrinth of men's desires,
> Suck in the millions in the caverned streets
> Dazzled by this, by that, distraction to the eyes,
> But tasted seem to scald me, like the heat.
> And yet, I know that here the Holy Grail
> May sail across my vision like a pale.
> Sun, when the skies are darkened by a gale!
> The caverns yawn and fall as death, the walls
> Where men are daily sold in juke-boxed stalls.
> Here many scratch at any straw that seems
> To pledge fulfillment to one's littlest dreams.[11]

This feeling of alienation, of not belonging in this city, is present in the "Additional Poems" written in the same period as the poems in *The City and the Thread of Light*. "Filipino Poet at Angkor Wat," a meditation in unrhymed hexameters, is an evocation of the religious faith, the proud ambitions, and the ultimate decline and death, the last symbolized by

---

[10] *The City and the Thread of Light*, passim.
[11] "In This City Dreamed by Augustine?," 28.

the crumblings of the rocks at Angkor, swallowed up by wild forests until rediscovered, to the amazed eyes of tourists and archaeologists. The tragedy is what it is; the human adventure is vaulting to a peak, then plunging to obscurity. Jayavarman VII, driven to religious zeal by leprosy, impoverished his land with feverish conquests, and the megalomaniac building and maintenance of great religious sanctuaries, such as Angkor Thom.

> For even empires yield to dust.
> Oblivion is a stone defaced.
> The lotus wilted in the lakes.
> This is a city full of ghosts.
>
> All that remains of human pride
> Crumbles in ruins, bit by bit.
> The idiom of the night is heard:
> Glory shrinks in the shroud of death.[12]

SIC TRANSIT GLORIA MUNDI. Thus passes the glory of the world. Nothing is permanent in this world, and everything shall pass away and fade. Some people seek the will of God upon their knees and venture upon mystic waters, like the Augustinian friar Andrés de Urdaneta.

> Did I, who is admiral of the seas,
> Really believe the Dove would gyre above my head
> And leave me as a gift a stigmata?
> Still, God has need of soldiers, for the tread
> On empire mapped out by their Majesties
> Prepares the chrismed chalice of wine and blood.[13]

In the poem about Osei-san, the feeling of alienation is crystallized in a monologue. Rizal's Japanese sweetheart is a romantic exile in this valley of tears. Demetillo has put into the poem the memories and thoughts of women loved and lost. The patriotic element is minimal in work.

---

[12] "Filipino Poet at Angkor Wat," 63
[13] "Andrés de Urdaneta," 78.

The autumn leaves upon the boughs of trees,
Shaking the leaves like lacy handkerchiefs
That flutter gently on the formal sand
Raked on the garden of the city parks.
The heart remembers only memories,
Like gestures of farewell waved by the hand.
The heart is cold, doused all the living sparks.
Doused also all the ancient ecstasies!

One walks along the lanes and thoughts arise,
Tenuous as mists that cling upon the trees.
One sees the changing clouds between the boughs.
How far away they seem, all out of reach.
To dissipate—the dreams of autumn skies.
A breeze puffs them away and leaves a pall
Weighing upon the scene. The leafless peach
Shakes in the listless wind before it dies.

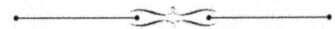

I feel the wintry frost along the street.
Chrysanthemums are withered on their stalks
That once were proud flames on their brilliant rows.
The city is a hive of loneliness.
The yellow lamplight pale upon my feet.
The joy of spring-time flew away with crows.
I clasp my bosom with my memories,
But in this autumn, I can feel no heat![14]

Man has landed on the moon. Is this an indication that he will subdue the galaxies? Will this give him fulfillment in this life? The poem on the American landing on the moon is not just another laudatory poem. The poet tries to relate the event to the human condition, the failures of man's dream of justice, peace, love, and faith. The poetic tone is not overly optimistic, for the wickedness of man is a deadly, devious thing. It ends with a warning or what appears to be a hint of it.

---

[14] "Osei-san," 66-67.

> There, man, perhaps, will find respite
> From all the warfares in their blood.
> There they will try to build anew
> The dreams of justice, grace and love,
> Or perish from the mushroom dusts.[15]

The city of man is a prelude to the city of God. Man is doomed if he takes this life on earth as final. There are many sufferings in this world and calamities, all indicating that earth is not the ultimate heaven. Demetillo is very Christian in his belief in the parousia, the second coming of Christ when the world will end, and man will be judged. There is no peace on earth in the strict sense. Like the faithful steward in the Gospel, man must always be watchful and use the city of man as a temporary stopover in his journey to the city of God.

> Sleep not, sleep not, there is no peace on earth.
> The world awaits the final holocaust,
> A cloud burst that will burn a prostrate earth,
> Inured in these decades for catastrophes.
> Sleep not, sleep not, there is no peace on earth.

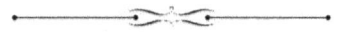

> Even lyrics charged with apocalypse,
> Now celebrate the final end, the burning earth;
> And man, wolf to his brothers, bares his teeth,
> Cornered by the rabid hates of centuries.
> Here, burrow in a hole beneath the earth![16]

The spiritual state of the land is at its lowest ebb, giving the poet reason to mourn.[17] The poet is aware of faces around him, but in a blurred way, for

---

[15] "The Astronauts," 73.

[16] "Theme from Saint Theresa Brought Up to Date," 75.

[17] Letter of Ricaredo Demetillo to Gilbert Luis R. Centina III, OSA, dated November 27, 1972, Quezon City.

the crowd is anonymous, rushing or spurting or swirling about and then dispersing like all multitudes.

> One says hello, then later says goodbye,
> Shaking a limp hand moist with the sweat,
> The dirt of bodies smudged by cindered soot.
> The city thunders on a maddened pace;
> And all the people are subject to that rush:
> Pleasure and gain, the laws of kiosk and mart.[18]

Nevertheless, the poet also sees salvation in the city of man. In his "Poem for a Young Priest," he thinks that God, after all, is not indifferent. It is the duty of the servants of the Lord, like the young priest, to guide people to salvation by teaching them to fix their minds on heavenly things.

> I like to think the God we serve
> Listens, not in indifference,
> But searches for the lost; and we,
> My friend, go to the puddled ways
> To teach the young men and to lead
> Children lost in the asphalt maze.[19]

Enlightenment comes with the desire to reach that other city, the city of God, which is the perfection of the city of man. One needs an ideal to reach this heavenly City; Demetillo finds this ideal in Jesus Christ. By acknowledging a being higher than man at par with the Creator, Demetillo has woven a theological outlook that is deeply religious and purely Christian.

THREAD THROUGH THE LABYRINTH. Illumination comes with a glimpse of what lies beyond the earthly city. The uncertainty of the poem "Lost" at the start of the collection is now eclipsed by slivers of light coming from the verses in the latter portion. The time is no longer the fifties when

---

[18] "The Shibboleths of the Mob," 47.
[19] "Poem for a Young Priest," 54.

"rebellious" accusations against the Church are made by one treading the labyrinth, as in *La Via*; this is the decade of the seventies, and the thread of light serves as the lamp of someone passing through the maze.

> We have to grope through so much dirt and grime
> And senselessness to reach our home again;
> And there's no one to guide us through the caves
> But our home-sickness, which is thirst and prod.
> We never quite can lose the thread however dark,
> Dark, steep or numb the labyrinth, unless
> Of course, we quit to lie down on the ground,
> And ice forms round the heart to freeze it in.[20]

His own "homesickness" guides man in his earthly stint. The heart thirsts for a place to rest; with this thirst, man will never get lost looking for the city of God unless he ceases to help himself and becomes spiritually dumb.

The other life is home. Happiness is God the loving Father welcoming his child home. God will wipe away all tears in heaven; God is yearning, waiting Form.

> There! Now we hear the birds sing once again.
> The light-girt hedges where they sing is home,
> Beyond the steep road that we all have climbed;
> Behind us forever left the dread we bore.
>
> And look, there wits my radiant Father's arms,
> I run and clasp that yearning waiting Form,
> I feel the winds of spring return again.
> See, there's a daisy and the robins sing![21]

The longing for the infinite proves that there is an indefinite Being, God. The poem of Saint Francis of Assisi is significant because it is here that Demetillo, on more mature premises, synthesizes his religious and artistic pre-suppositions. He does it aligned with the larger, more comprehensive

---

[20] "Thread Through the Labyrinth," 51.
[21] Ibid.

vision, which includes faith, love, and beauty—all attributes of God. Because Saint Francis is, for him, the great troubadour poet, he uses his figure in this poem of faith. If *La Via* was over-compensation, inviting hubris, this one poem and all that will follow it are restitution. Since he wrote *La Via*, it is with this poem that he has returned in humility and faith to the fold of the Son, Lord of Light and Love, whom he here celebrates:

> The saint emerges from a dark-mouthed cave
> Made softer by a trellis where the vines
> Attest to life deep-rooted in the earth.
> The figure has advanced on shoeless feet.
>
> Against ascetic rocks, the figure seems
> Fragile, as all created things are frail.
> But glory is an aureole round his head.
> Severe, the gown is softened by the sun.
>
> What is he doing on this altitude?
> The sun is shining, nimbus full of love,
> Caressing fields and houses with its warmth.
> The trees burst into bloom and bear their fruits.
>
> The world is vast, vast like an infinite;
> But God has touched a man's heart with His love.
> This is a poet praising dawn and dark,
> And all things, like the birds, the moss and weed.
>
> See, there's a spring that bubbles from a rock.
> It is the sluice of Grace that nurtures earth.
> The day has dappled all the hills with Light
> And led the saint to this ecstatic height.
>
> The patient ass that waits to take its load,
> Like men who work at industry to trade,
> Crops at the succulent tufts of grass, a bird
> Listens to the poet's joyous praise.
> Love is the Good that we must celebrate.
> See, all the verdurous boughs unfurl in love.
> Above the hilltop, glory is a blaze,
> And Brother Francis starts to chant his praise.

> O living Light that subjugates the dark
> And makes it serve the miracles of God,
> Bless now your Saint whose ecstasies are shared
> By all who know the Son and walk in Love.[22]

"Love, love, and love. Give, give, and give." Love, genuinely charged with light, creates patterns that harmonize the mind. Illumination culminates at the Cultural Center, where a ballet show and a one-person painting exhibit are going on, and at San Agustín Church, where an Augustinian guide who is a poet speaks about the glory of the past. The Cultural Center stands for art; San Agustín Church symbolizes the ageless Rock of man's spirituality. "Eros clasps Psyche, Psyche swoons with love" at the ballet dance at the Cultural Center; "purged of that baneful pride that dazzled men," the seminarians in San Agustín sow the seeds that grow and multiply in love.[23] The Holy Grail is found in man himself, and man is capable of lighting his candle so that the other candle lighted by the rest of his fellowmen, right in this very City, will be light and life for the spirit.

> And we, my brothers lost, now found by Him,
> Who limps with wounded feet to seek His own,
> Let's seek the alleys and the hells that hive
> This City, bringing light, where still the dim
> Dark fetters millions, weighed by cares like stone!
> Go, go, my brothers, and urge the dead to live![24]

SALVATION IS FOR EVERYONE. It is the duty of the enlightened to spread the gospel of salvation and to enlighten, in turn, those who are still buried in ignorance. Just as there is a resurrection of the dead, so is a redemption of the living. Demetillo, more than ever, places salvation history right in the very city of man. Each enlightened human being is to be the apostle of love and light. Some men gain merit: by enlightening those who are in the dark; others are occasions of merit by their example; both pass through the city of light. It is a reiteration of the familiar theme: man is God's instrument in his divine plan.

---

[22] "Saint Francis in Ecstasy," 52-53.

[23] *The City and the Thread of Light*, passim.

[24] "The Grail: A Postlude," 59.

II. THE REDEEMED LIFE

Lazarus, Troubadour consists of seventy-seven poems which the poet has written in a span of seven days. It is a celebration of the redeemed life, based on Lazarus in the New Testament as the archetype. Demetillo assumes that he whom Jesus raised from the dead was a poet celebrating his chance for a second life.

TROUBADOUR OF THE LORD. The poems are autobiographical. After his rebellious attacks on the Church in *La Via*, the poet is Lazarus emerging from his unbelief, discovering and finding the way to his highest self.

> There is a quill engrafted to my thumb.
> It's thirty years this miracle has grown
> A white and feathery plume that, dipped in ink,
> Mixed from my crimson blood and the fiery air,
> Writes all the poems that astonish men.[25]

"Thirty years" is magic or religious number for the poet. When he writes this poem, Demetillo has been writing for thirty years, and the time now is post-Vatican II. His friendship at the time of the Lazarus poem with an Augustinian deacon may be significant to his spiritual growth as a poet. "Sometimes," says Demetillo in one of his letters to the religious, "I smile to myself that you have been sent by God to me so that my poetry will gain a new dimension...."[26] The following poem, addressed to the spiritual founder of the Augustinian Order, is very revealing:

> I don't invite the tigers, Augustine,
> For week-end visits and such things.

---

[25] "There Is a Quill Engrafted to My Thumb," *Lazarus, Troubadour*, 1. "Write all poems that astonish" is an advice that puts in black and white Demetillo's obsession to be immortalized. All poems considered in this section are to be found in the same work.

[26] To Gilbert Luis R. Centina III, OSA, dated March 3, 1973, Quezon City. In another letter to the same, he says: "My spiritual awareness has deepened much since our friendship started. And I am aware that your own self has progressed a lot, too, since your knowing me." (October 25, 1973, Quezon City.)

> I bed with them and know their stripes,
> Their deadly fangs and spring.
>
> Inviting them is dilettante.
> To live with them is mastery.
> With love and care but sternest whip
> To make them kneel to me.
>
> I know that pow'r that shook old Blake
> And other things beside:
> The sudden leap across my mind,
> The supple grace and glide!
>
> How shall I prove this to the world
> And you, dear Augustine?
> Here, see the scars on heart, on brow:
> The proofs of discipline![27]

In the Troubadour poems, the style is stripped of almost all adjectives. The poet wishes to show man (Lazarus) bare of all extraneous elements as he stands before the Lord of Light. The style is as simple, dignified, and direct as possible: no involved sentences, no pretentious language. For God sees man naked, without masks.

> I am a troubadour
> Dressed in a colored coat,
> Dancing with light step, so,
> Singing what God has wrought!
>
> Marvel is at my eyes
> And praise is at my tongue.
> Life is a gift. Then, live
> As flowers the whole day long!
> Why gather so much gold,
> With fret and weariness?
> Walk in the warmth or cold
> To find pure happiness!

---

[27] "I Don't Invite the Tigers, Augustine," 10. In an interview, Demetillo disclosed that this particular poem is a rebuttal of José Garcia Villa's invitation to tigers for a weekend in one of Villa's untitled poems.

> Sure, man declines and dies
> And man lies with the sod.
> But death frights not at all
> To those who live with God![28]

For all its simplicity, the poem has power and profundity. The poet is God's troubadour, singing what God wants him to sing. Awed by God's grandeur, he sings his praises. Life is God's gift to man, who must use it well. Christ's exhortation to have faith in the biblical passage on the lilies of the field becomes familiar. Man must remain detached from earthly preoccupations because the world will not last forever, and another life awaits beyond. One who walks with God does not have to fear death, for his reward is in the other life. It is this kind of poetry, one may surmise, which awakens those who are aware of the life of the spirit. Such awareness is a gift from the good Lord. Lazarus, as the troubadour of the Lord, sings of the inner life:

> The lowly pots and pans,
> Of cheap ware made,
> May shine,
> Scoured by a maid
> For daily use!
> I, who am not
> Exactly pan or pot,
> Though mired with mud,
> Stand
> A noble man—
> Washed by God
> For sacred use![29]

Demetillo's image of the redeemed man is clear: he is noble because God washed him. It reiterates his preface to the Troubadour poems: "Man must stand as Son of God with poise and dignity, not slinking by because of his fears and anxieties. Sin is not central to our Faith; it is Love that under-

---

[28] "I Am a Troubadour," 4.
[29] "A Troubadour of My Lord," 5.

stands, heals, and forgives."³⁰ The challenge of *La Via* is hurried all over again, but now in a milder, peaceable tone; the voice is that of a prodigal son who has returned to his father.³¹

GRACE BAFFLES THE MICROSCOPE. Reverend David A. Sobrepeña, the Protestant chaplain of the University of the Philippines around the time *Lazarus, Troubadour* was published, has warm praise for the poetry collection: "These professionally-crafted poems are also the outpouring of a human soul; faith welled up with such force in the poet's heart that it would no longer contain the joy of the experience of God's grace...The poems reflect new life after time spent in the valley of the shadow of death. The economy of line and passionate intensity mark these poems. They attempt to bridge the chasm between evil and good, light and darkness, holy and unholy....."³²

For Demetillo, the miracle of grace is such that it baffles the microscope. The miracle uses a mundane object but ends with spiritual enlightenment.

> One must of need be agonized
> By loves, by guilts, by phlegm;
> And if the frail flesh does not crack,
> One graduates to: a Gem!
> One moment, one will crawl about.
> The next, the chains are free
> And poems burst upon the page:
> Grace, brilliant mystery!³³

---

³⁰ "A Preface," ix.

³¹ Is there mysticism in it? Demetillo writes: "I am glad that you find *La Via* challenging and really not heretical. I mistrust, of course, the idea that I am a mystic of sorts, though there have been certain experiences of mine that appear somewhat strange and, to my rational mind, a little baffling. I say mistrust for in such matters, God can easily become the Devil, and complacency can result from such an experience. That is why, one has to check with one's reason on certain emotional experiences that are out of the usual. To go into the depths can be courting disaster, even to the point of becoming insane. Yet, of course, one must meet that risk, for how can one achieve profundity except by diving into the depths of life?" (Letter to Gilbert Luis R. Centina III, OSA, dated July 26, 1973, Quezon City.)

³² Critical comment, *Lazarus, Troubadour*, outside back cover.

³³ "Grace Baffles Microscope," 8.

The spiritual predicament of modern man is that he cannot find joy and grace because he cannot love others, himself, and God. Until love becomes a light that warms one's dawn, one is alienated from oneself, others, and God. Demetillo is obviously in love with his work. His, therefore, is a miracle of creativity. His poems prove the catholicity of genuine poetry; he should be read for his works' universal truth and beauty. His poems are a loving search for readers and lovers; more and more people shall find in them the patent for their spiritual strivings, the release from their agony of soul.

> Feeling this flame of grace,
> I cannot help but share
> It with those who mope
> In bleak cells of despair.[34]

The paradigms of grace that form the bulk of *Lazarus, Troubadour*, are Demetillo's affirmation of the essential validity of the Christian outlook. Two things, however, have deeply troubled the poet, as he explains in his preface. First: "Christianity, especially in the Gospels and in subsequent pronouncements, ignores the artistic experience or, at the most, grudgingly makes passing concessions to them, with the result that, in the majority of cases, the artists and those who study and lovingly understand them, have been alienated from the Christian religion to the loss and impoverishment of the latter, and, no doubt, to the frustrations, guilts, and fury of these artists, whose works we tend to separate from those we term 'religious.'" Second: "The other aspect involves the fear of the Body as 'unholy and source of temptation,' together with that whole corpus of experiences which is symptomatically called *sensual*. The Church teaches the Fatherhood of God, but it politely but firmly elides or represses the fecund male sensuality of God's creative function, which all Nature semaphores to us, if only we have the eyes and the mind to apprehend."[35]

In the Eucharist of love, Demetillo's poetic vision entwines the sensual with the holy "to dance the rhythm, pure as snow, but warm to bless

---

[34] "Feeling This Flame of Grace," 9.
[35] "A Preface," viii-ix.

mankind." He walks ahead of Christ, then Christ walks ahead of him, and from this familiarity between the Divine and the mortal, true liberty is born beneath the radiant cross. What has the Lord to do with dumps? The following poem resolves the seemingly incongruent mixture of the pure with the impure:

> What has my Lord to do with dumps,
> The leak and lank of poverty,
> And all the aches and coughs?
> I asked rebukingly.
>
> My Lord turned, "Oh, my Lazarus,"
> He said in sad degree,
> "The doctor loves not pus.
> He seeks a cautery.
>
> "I do not like to see men stoop
> Or hear them sigh and moan
> Or waste down to the grave
> Or weighed down by a stone.
>
> "I like to see men leap with joy!
> That is their heritage:
> That they should live in full
> And reach a noble age.
>
> "Once, too, dear Lazarus,
> You were like one of them.
> Were you not strait-jacketed
> And buried in a tomb?
> "But I subdued your dark
> And called you back—
> That I may call you Friend,
> Freed from a deathly Rock!"
>
> And so, rebuked by Him,
> I turned a little shamed;
> Then stood and ran to help
> The sick, the maimed.[36]

---

[36] "What Has My Lord to Do with Dumps," 14.

Demetillo's concept of God is a dispenser of grace. God hates sin but loves the sinner; he wants man to be happy through his grace. Sin is spiritual death, as Lazarus' entombment signifies.

Mary Magdalene, who has had seven devils cast out of her by Jesus Christ, can be any woman living at present, dissatisfied by grasping at all the sensuous-sensual aspects of modern life.

> The Magdalene and I:
> Two of a kind,
> Seeking to find
> God beneath the crust
> That cannot satisfy—
> And tastes like dust.[37]

The poetic subject hits a central predicament in modern life. Clarity, unity, and grace wedded to tensile strength make the Magdalene a great poem. The line schemes are most varied and highly interesting. Demetillo's preferred poetic form is usually the iambic pentameter, but there are many unusual variations this time.

The world is transfigured by Demetillo's experience of Light in his poem on the Blessed Virgin Mary.

> I sing of Mary, full of grace
> Who walked upon the lawn and felt the Light
> Streaming in splendor on her dazzled sight
> And seemed to her a lover's face!
> The gentle winds undid her lace;
> And while the Highest overshadowed her,
> She lay, a slender Virgin, young and fair.
> Hail, Mary, full of grace!
>
> "My soul doth magnify the Lord."
> Her words were wafted on the air with wings.
> Indeed, the Lord had done to her great things:
> Holy, the everlasting Word!

---

[37] "The Magdalene and I," 15.

"Behold the handmaid of the Lord!"
There was a holy hush around this maiden;
And in her hazel eyes shone the Light of Heaven:
She who had bowed in meek accord!

How was the luminance to fade
From all the Universe which God has made?
There was undying radiance in this Maid
And on the vale where lambkins played.

All the generations call Thee blest!"
The angels sang and all shone full of light
Though soon would fade the day, and Night
Would lull this Virgin to her rest.[38]

In one of his letters, the poet explains the genesis of this poem:

> The "Hail, Mary" poem was done half an hour ago. Before that I was reading from Luke's Gospel, the first few chapters; and of a sudden, I began taking notes about some lines that struck me as especially lovely and meaningful; and out of these I created the poem only. I was afraid that I might introduce some indelicacies which would repeal some sensibilities, to do a most delicate creation of a pure song: Catholic, as you would say. Anyway, I am sending you the carbon copy of the miraculous thing. I think it is holy.[39]

The author intended this poem to be holy, which makes it different from his *La Via* poems on the same theme. More cautious, he describes Mary's overshadowing by the Holy Spirit with spiritual finesse. By his admission, we can call this particular poem not only catholic but genuinely Catholic.

Imprisoned by the dark, the poet retained a memory of wings. He who wrote rebellious sonnets now writes a "holy" sonnet after being healed by the chrism of faith. But for the grace of the Lord, he might have remained the man who coughs all night. Martha nags, but she is kind and good,

---

[38] "Hail, Mary, Full of Grace," 52.
[39] Letter of Ricaredo Demetillo to Gilbert Luis R. Centina III, OSA, dated September 13, 1973, Quezon City. The poet enclosed with this letter his poem, "The Magdalene and I."

able to fill the needs in her guts and loins. God uses no force so man can succumb to his grace. God's grace is encompassing. He chooses the humble for his uses. The poet is sensual as the dark Adam in his body snarls. He celebrates God's grace by honoring man's fullness. The human body, as seen by Demetillo, is God's repository of his graces. By not starving this body, by disciplining it, or using it to the full, man passes to perfect enlightenment and becomes God's child of grace, able to walk straight and live his creative life to the glorification of the Creator.[40]

AFTER ENLIGHTENMENT. After enlightenment, what? The poet is grateful to his Maker. In his relationship with the Creator, he realizes that man is a frail vessel after the Fall. He must confront the evil within him; there are human sufferings he must affirm. The distance from self to Christ is from North to South; man is a mere animal unless Christ sheds luster on the heart and mind to exorcise the dim.[41] As the enlightened troubadour personified in Lazarus, the poet must celebrate the Light with the wisdom won by grace. He must not sing for himself but for God, "whose accents stir these songs to rouse the blood."[42] Looking closely, he sees that, in every man, Lucifer is there, not only Christ. Enlightenment enables the pygmy Christ to tower over Lucifer "to shape this living *I*."[43] That is the miracle in man which only Christ is capable of performing.

Demetillo does not dare to divide the unholy from the holy. A saint may commit murder; conversely, a profligate may become the holiest of the wise and the wisest of the holy, as did Saint Augustine. Sanctity is for everybody within anybody's reach, and all men are predestined to heaven unless they choose hell through their own will.

> We are not pigs or slaves, but Sons with Christ,
> Who was banged upon that gibbet, Calvary,
> That He may pour the ichor of His love,
> To heal the sundered body, Humanity.[44]

---

[40] *Lazarus, Troubadour, passim.*
[41] Ibid.
[42] "No, Not for the Love of Self I Sing," 63.
[43] "When I look Close Enough," 64.
[44] "The Christ Has Blessed the Life We Live," 78.

Christ guides all men to eternal happiness. Christ who loved the Magdalene, with his lover's eyes, healed men with his vitality, blesses the life men live. With Christ's death, God is glorified. The radiant Cross is the key to man's glory. All else is vanity and dross.

> The Glory and Majesty of God
> Streams from the radiant Cross.
> So, I, God's Troubadour, cling to It.
> All else is Vanity and Dross.[45]

After enlightenment, the poet returns to the world to proclaim God's mercy and grace. God is the guest and constant friend as the poet takes his place in the academe to teach men their worthy end: God himself.

> I go back to the world and take my place,
> A humble one, a teacher who can stir
> The seeds within youth's mind, that I may see
> The illumination on each face
> Brighten the corridors and halls, like space
> Lit by the Sun, all marvelous![46]

Through the archetypal figure of Lazarus rising from the dead, Demetillo has, to borrow the words of Philippine National Artist for Literature Francisco Arcellana, become "the poet of eternal morality."[47]

The City and the Thread of Light and *Lazarus, Troubadour* are written many years after the Second Vatican Council. The poems sparkle with enlightenment. The poet likens himself to Lazarus, raised from the tomb through the mercy of God, celebrating the Redeemed Life.

In the City poems, Demetillo celebrates the city of man half in hate and half in love. Half in contempt because the City can obstruct man's journey to the spiritual. Half in love because the Holy Grail may yet be found in

---

[45] "Summons: The Final Paradigm," 84.
[46] "After Enlightenment," 61.
[47] Critical comment, *Lazarus, Troubadour,* outside back cover.

this City. Restlessness can prod man to higher things. By realizing that this life offers nothing but transitory joy, man yearns for that other City in the Great Beyond where all dreams are fulfilled. The City poems culminate in the Cultural Center of the Philippines, where a ballet dance and a one-person art exhibit by a painter are taking place, and in San Agustín Church, the oldest stone church in the country, where the seminarians of the Augustinian Order are learning the lesson of humility. Enlightenment comes like a thread of light as the artistic fuses with the religious to create a harmony of mind and body.

The feeling of loss experienced in the terrestrial domain finds a contrapuntal force in the blending of the religious and the artistic, and the familiar places no longer become so but blaze with ethereal colors in anticipation of the Infinite.

In the Troubadour poems, Lazarus becomes the archetypal symbol of the redeemed life. Salvation is for everyone, holy and unholy alike. Sin is death, but through the mercy of God, one is reconciled from the tomb to start a new life of repentance and service to the Creator. Sin is not central to faith; it is love that understands, heals, and forgives. The creative function of man must be appropriately exploited to glorify the nature of his Creator.

When he faces his Creator, he should strip himself naked of all superficialities. As God's adopted son, he must walk with dignity and poise, aware of the love of God, his loving Father. Predestined to eternal joy, he can be doomed only through free will. God's grace is gratuitous for man to reciprocate. He who is given a second chance to live spiritually all over again is God's troubadour, his instrument in proclaiming his infinite mercy and boundless grace.

Enlightenment comes to Demetillo after three decades of writing poetry. Man, he says, is a mixture of both Christ and Lucifer. Christ's greatest miracle occurs in man when Christ towers over Lucifer and, out of the weak mortal, makes a troubadour whose greatest glory is to praise the Creator and lead his fellowmen to the ultimate end, God himself.

CHAPTER V

CONCLUSION

The merit of Ricaredo Demetillo as a poet is not in the poetry of his subject but the subject of his poetry. Our chief purpose in this study is to present him as a religious poet *sui generis*. Religious elements have always been present in his work from when he left a Protestant seminary at the outbreak of World War II in favor of a literary career until at least the mid-nineteen seventies while holding a professorial chair at the University of the Philippines. He has successfully combined his literary pursuits with his career in academia.

The early poems of Demetillo are poems of doubt. The Supreme Being looms as a father figure forced on him by his elders. He rebels against false values and fake conventions. The seeming lack of faith in the poet is understandable since, at this early period, he is trying to find himself and, in the process God. Frustrated, he leaves the seminary. His spiritual crisis leads him to produce that kind of religious poetry in the sense that it questions the existence of God. God is sought and known in the negatives.

Darkness leads to an intense search, a spiritual journey that commences in the hell portion of human life, progresses through purgatory and ends in the acceptance of life through love. To Demetillo, the institutionalized Church is one of the most repressive agents of society. By looking down on sex, the Church has produced sexually-imbalanced people incapable of loving and responding to love. Intense sorrow pervades the family circle because of the absence of love. To the poet, man's spiritual and creative fullness can be achieved to the fullest only through the proper exercise of their psycho-physical functions, especially the sexual. Guilts, anxieties, and even madness result from an over-rigid denial of such functions.

The Church, by commercializing religion, ceases to be the haven of the spiritually sick and burdened. Religions mushroom everywhere; each one points to heaven and claims to be the way. The poet considers lip-service piety and hypocritical morality as no better than those of the pagans of yore. Devotions that border on the courageous and the ridiculous only alienate people from the Church. The God whom the Church presents is a product of monetary considerations. The ecclesiastics have lost their moral credibility through the theology of candles and plaster saints, which gives rise to simony. By leveling his attack on the institutionalized Church, Demetillo acts as a religious reformer.

In his spiritual journey, the poet finds that civilizations rise and fall through excesses of the flesh. The flesh, the poet reasons out, must be used with moderation without denying the spirit. Agape and Eros must complement each other, not war against each other. Only through their harmony does the flesh yield to the spirit. But when the flesh is stifled, the spirit suffers. The golden mean of the Greeks is a healthy compromise.

Religion in the Philippines suffers from corruption within and without. Superstition has not been eradicated, and people are trained to say Amen without being taught how to live their religion according to their convictions. Religious awareness, necessary for peace of conscience, is lacking.

God is the God of the living, not of the dead. Heaven and hell are within man himself. Through self-knowledge, man regains his lost paradise. Love alone heals and forgives.

In art, Demetillo finds the immanent God through his kinship with fellow artists. Depending on his psyche, the poet reflects, and the artist writes about his age. Art is calvary; the artist participates in Christ's calvary. Restless in spirit, the artist can rest only in God because he alone can fill the void within his heart. The artist is God's instrument in this world to proclaim and glorify him. Through the life and art of the artist, God is completed in the world of the tangibles.

As an artist, Demetillo eschews art for art's sake and art as propaganda. He deals with man in man's totality. Aside from celebrating both Filipino and foreign artists, he deals with the common man in society. Christ is the highest ideal man can attain, but the ordinary man is a scarecrow in society.

The artist feels an affinity with the poor, having known human suffering himself. He is a free man. He speaks for his people honestly, for the truth sets men free. In fine, God in whose image and likeness man is created is the Alpha and Omega of all arts, for he lets the Spirit work in a manner that the Spirit wants.

After seeing the changes in the Church brought about by Vatican II, Demetillo changed his outlook without necessarily repudiating the premises of his past works. His journey through the City is not uncertain, rambling as in the earlier poems, but purposeful and definitive. The City is familiar yet unfamiliar, celebrated half in hate and half in love. It is the prelude to that City Eternal where God is enthroned and the blessed share his glory. The city of man is not the final resting place; it is a labyrinth in which man loses himself but achieves glory after his fall because God forgives if man repents. Loneliness and alienation punctuate the true path. But in the end, man prevails if he lets Eros clasp with Agape if he can dominate his passions and make his spirit sober. Homesickness for the Eternal City is man's beacon light. By fixing his gaze upon the City of God, man disentangles himself from the snares that pave the labyrinth. Demetillo's religiosity here is marked by his belief in the parousia, the second coming of Christ, and his acceptance of the next life. For Demetillo, the spirit is immortal.

And because the spirit is immortal, there is a resurrection of the dead. Lazarus is a poet redeemed by Christ. This archetypal symbol is also autobiographical. Death is the wages of sin. The poet wishes to show man stripped of all extraneous elements as he stands before the Lord of Light. Man must recognize his minuteness in order to be redeemed. After his enlightenment, he must sing of God's mercy and justice. The redeemed man is noble because God washed him. "Man must stand as Son of God with poise and dignity, not slinking by because of his fears and anxieties. Sin is not central to our faith; it is Love that understands, heals, forgives."

After man's journey, God his Father is ready to welcome him as his son. The greatest miracle Christ performed on earth was the resurrection of Lazarus, who, seized by God, could not contain the joy of living in God and sang of this miracle of miracles within his heart.

In all this, Demetillo shows himself to be a religious poet. First, he begins in doubt and darkness to attain wisdom. Next, he undertakes a spiritual journey that proves that no institution, not even the Church, can save man from the utter loss of his soul except God's love. Then, he finds God immanent in his kinship with artists and fellow human beings. Finally, he finds redemption through the mercy of God, whose goodness he, in the archetypal symbol of Lazarus, sings.

In his poetry, Demetillo has always dealt with God as a loving Father, ready to forgive. His relationship with the Creator has always been familiar, yet, he asserts that because God is the dispenser of grace, man must respond. This is the pivotal point in the Creator-creature relationship on which Demetillo's religiosity as a poet hinges.

BIBLIOGRAPHY

I. Books

Abbot, Walter M., SJ (gen. ed.). *The Documents of Vatican II.* New York: Guild Press, 1969.

Attwater Donald. *The Penguin Dictionary of Saints.* England: Penguin Books, Inc., 1965.

Bourke, Vernon J. (ed.). *The Essential Augustine.* New York: The New American Library, 1964.

Carbonell, Rolando. *Beloved. A Treasury of Love Poems.* Manila: 1968.

Casper, Leonard. *Six Filipino Poets.* Manila: Benipayo Press, 1954.

—. *The Wounded Diamond.* Manila: Bookmark, 1964.

Centina, Gilbert Luis III R., OSA. *Glass of Liquid Truths.* Makati: The Augustinian Fathers, 1974.

Demetillo, Ricaredo. *Barter in Panay.* Quezon City: University of the Philippines Press, 1961.

—. *Daedalus and Other Poems.* n.p.: 1962.

—. *La Via: A Spiritual Journey.* Quezon City: University of the Philippines Press, 1958.

—. *Lazarus, Troubadour.* Quezon City: New Day Publishers, 1974.

—. *Masks and Signature.* Quezon City: University of the Philippines Press, 1968.

—. *No Certain Weather.* Quezon City: Guinhalinan Press, 1956.

—. *The Authentic Voice of Poetry.* Quezon City: University of the Philippines Press, 1962.

—. *The City and the Thread of Light.* Quezon City: University of the Philippines Press, 1972.

—. *The Scare-Crow Christ.* Quezon City: University of the Philippines Press, 1972.

Espino, Federico Licsi Jr. *Burnt Alphabets.* Manila: Pioneer Press, 1969.

Engle, Paul (ed.). *Midland.* New York: Random House, 1961.

Hufana, A.G. *Notes on Poetry.* Quezon City: University of the Philippines Press, 1973.

Maramba, Asuncion David (ed.). *Philippine Contemporary Literature.* Fourth Edition. Manila: Bookmark, 1974.

Merton, Thomas. *The Living Bread.* New York: Farrar, Straus & Giraux, 1956.

Murphy, Rosalie. *Contemporary Poets of the English Language.* London: St. James Press, 1970.

Noon, William T., SJ. *Poetry and Prayer.* New Jersey: Rutgers University Press, 1967.

Robinson, John A.T. *In the End God.* London: Fontana Books, 1968.

Rubio, Pedro, OSA. *Take and Read (The Augustinian Answer).* Manila: Arnoldus Press Inc., 1976.

Santa Romana, M.L. (ed.). *Sinaglahi.* Quezon City: Writers Union of the Philippines, 1965.

Schoonfield, Hugh J. *A History of Biblical Literature.* New York: The American Library, 1962.

Torres, Emmanuel (ed.). *An Anthology of Poems 1965-1974.* Manila: Bureau of National and Foreign Information, 1975.

Trese, Leo J. *Guide to Christian Living.* Indiana: Fides Publishers, Inc. 1973.

Tuvera, Juan C. (ed.). *Katha I.* Manila: Katha Edition, 1956.

Viray, Manuel A. *Heart of the Island.* Manila: University Pub. Co., 1947.

Walsh, Thomas. *The World's Catholic Anthology.* New York: Macmillan and Co., 1947.

White, Helen C. *The Metaphysical Poets.* New York: Macmillan and Co., 1935.

II. Periodical Literature

Bautista, Cirilo F., "Philippine Poetry in English," *Solidarity*, December 1970: 67-72.

Carrol, John J., "Magic and Religion," *Solidarity*, April 1968: 1-34.

Casper, Leonard, "A Haggle of Filipino Poets 1966-68," *Solidarity*, March 1969: 53-64.

Centina, Gilbert Luis III R., OSA, "Lazarus as a Poet," *Homelife*, November 1974: 38.

—. "On a Filipino Poet's 'Image of Man'," Philippine Priests' Forum, VI, 1, (March 1974): 12-16.

—. "The Image of Man in Ricaredo Demetillo," *Homelife*, October 1973: 29.

Centina, Louella Cecilia R., "The City and the Thread of Light," *Philwomanian*, September 1974: 5-6.

Cuadra, Jolico, "The Poets Unmasked," *Solidarity*, February 1969: 58-62.

Demetillo, Ricaredo, "Dimensions and Responsibilities of Philippine Literary Criticism," *The Literary Apprentice*, November 1974: 57-67.

—. "Filipino Artists in the Early 1970s," *Solidarity*, 1973: 41-48.

—. "Image of Man in Contemporary Art & Literature," *Humanities 4*: 41-48.

—. "Journey Into the Mist," *Solidarity*, March 1975: 66-111.

—. "Nationalism in the Plastic Arts," *Comment 3*, Second Quarter, (1957): 36-43.

—. "Nick Joaquin: A Dialogue," *Comment 1*, October 1956: 19-22.

—. "The Cripples," *Homelife*, April 1974: 38-41.

Espino, Federico Licsi Jr., "Poets New and Otherwise," *Archipelago*, III, 25, (1976): 30-33.

Jocano, F. Landa, "Maragtas: Fact or Fiction?," *Solidarity*, April 1968: 35-47.

Pineda, R.V., "Writer Draw Battle Lines," *U.P. Newsletter*, May 3, 1976: 6.

Tiempo, Edilberto K., "The Impact of New Criticism in the Philippines," *Solidarity*, December 1970: 52-57.

III. Holy Bible

The Jerusalem Bible. London: Darton, Longman & Todd, 1966.

IV. Unpublished

Centina, Gilbert Luis III R., OSA, "The Scare-Crow Image of Christ in Ricaredo Demetillo," critical essay.

Demetillo, Ricaredo. *The Autobiography of a Troubled Vision*. An autobiographical novel.

V. Online Sources

"Pope: Clericalism Distances the People from the Church," *en.radiovaticana.va*. Accessed November 12, 2017. *https://bit.ly/3rW5QpH*.

Guerrero, Amadis Ma., "Ricaredo Demetillo: Poet of Panay epics," *Philippines Graphics* magazine online. Accessed October 25, 2022. https://bit.ly/3FgMkMc.

Alegre, Edilberto N. and Fernandez, Doreen G., eds., "Ricaredo Demetillo," *Writers & Their Milieu* (Mandaluyong City: Anvil Publishing, 2012). Books.google.com. Accessed October 20, 2017. *https://bit.ly/3W1ZYJo*.

APPENDIX

Letters of Ricaredo Demetillo To Gilbert Luis R. Centina III

T1416 Area 14
U.P. Campus, Diliman[1]
November 27, 1972

Dear Gilbert,

I am a little confused as to how to address you! But I hope you don't mind my using your first name, which is quite distinctive.

Your poem to me touches my heart very much. It is a fine poem, by itself; and since it is about me, it has a double significance. Thank you for a very lovely thought.

Sometimes, when you are not busy, do come and visit at my place. You are always welcome, and we can "chew the rug," as the Americans would say. Besides, I want to hear how you almost got married! You know, of course, that to most of us mortals, marriage is a very acceptable thing, without any involvement in guilt, etc.

I am writing a lot nowadays—poems and prose. *The Diliman Review* is publishing my next book: *The Scare-Crow Christ*. The title poem deals with the very poor and most exploited. Christ is the highest men can attain; but in our society, the ordinary man is a scarecrow. But you can make your own metaphysical significances, versed as you are on the levels of meanings involved in metaphoric language.

I am writing more and more poems on the general theme of the City. The spiritual state in our land is at its lowest ebb; and this gives me reason to mourn. I may try to find a magazine to publish these long poems. When I do, I shall send one or two to your magazine, *Homelife*. I am also thinking of *Focus Philippines*.

---

[1] All letters were written by Ricaredo Demetillo from his home at the University of the Philippines campus unless otherwise stated.

Did you know that I'm writing a long autobiograpical novel? I have actually written about a third of the whole thing, but I'm dissatisfied with the results. This January, I shall have only three classes to teach; so possibly, I shall be able to write the other sections. By July, too, I shall be on a sabbatical leave for a whole year. Isn't that wonderful?

The martial law[2] cut the publications of several critical essays and poems. at *PIC*, at the *Asian Philippines Leader*, at *Fookien Times Yearbook*. Too bad!

Thanks again for writing. I always rejoice when friends are able to create the works they most long to write. And *salamat gid*[3] for "Compline."

Your friend,
Rick Demetillo

December 29, 1972

Dear Gilbert,

I owe you a letter, though I sent you copies of two recent poems to wish you well during the holiday season. I have enjoyed heartily your last long letter and am glad that you are continuing to write both fiction and poetry. As for me, I have really been lazying along for the past few days, after a hectic week of mechanical aspects of teaching: otherwise, it is a pleasant occupation with compensation other than monetary.

I sent you a copy of "cave poems," a re-interpretation of Plato's theme on the same subject. You can see how closely I have tried to follow his archetypal work, making it a philosophical work, with direct bearing to the poetic creativity of the poet. I have reservations about some of the lines; possibly I may need to re-word some sections.

I hope you had a good Christmas season. You have been on my mind the last few days, promising myself to write you. [Poet] Federico Licsi Espino came here one time when I was out, and he left behind a book of selected stories by Guy de Maupassant. I read "Ball of Fat," which is the great short

---

[2] President Ferdinand E. Marcos declared martial law all over the Philippines on September 21, 1972, and closed down newspapers and other publications.

[3] Hiligaynon for "thank you so much."

story by the master. During the last war, one of my comforts was reading him in several volumes, which I discovered in a friend's house. Now, after thirty years, I discover his limitation as a realist; his tendency to be dry and matter-of-fact, effective in a few stories but, perhaps, a little too dry for my taste. "Ball of Fat" is unusual, in that it penetrates deeply into the psychology of so-called respectable people, whose moral actuations make one wish to laugh in derision, something that Guy does in the brilliant story.

I am not yet certain about the summer writers workshop to be sponsored by the U.P. English department. If plans go though, we may hold it by April or early May. I'll keep you posted on this. You certainly deserve a place in such a workshop. I promise you my sponsorship if things go through properly.

After some hesitation, I sent Imelda[4] my poem about her. What I was curious about is her reaction to it. Possibly, she will just ignore it: it is, after all, the work of one not very familiar to her.

Do write again, and, if you have the time, come to the house. My friends are always welcome to our *nipa* hut. Send me any poems you may be working on or your efforts in the short story,

With my best wishes year to come,
Rick Demetillo

* * *

January 19, 1973

My dear Gilbert,

Just a note to tell you how nicely I feel about your praise for my new poems. Did you know that I have been writing fairly long poems lately, especially about the city and also about dancers and other artists? They are however not the kind to be published in such New Society[5] magazines as *Focus*. I feel that some of these poems have achieved dimensions of signif-

---

[4] Imelda Romualdez Marcos, first lady of the Philippines at that time.

[5] New Society is a phrase used by Philippine President Ferdinand E. Marcos to describe the country he envisioned with the reforms he introduced under martial law he declared in 1972.

icance that my earliest poems had not. Maybe, that is the result of greater maturity.

...Hufana[6] told me that the U.P. Workshop[7] may not be held this year, for there is no money for its expenses, as a result of the regents' decision not to hold summer classes. It's the summer classes that are supposed to be the source of the workshop money.

How about the Silliman workshop?[8] I'm sure that if the southern city's workshop will be held, you can easily get a spot. Just address your inquiries to Mrs. Edith Tiempo and also send some of your poems, so they have a basis for accepting you as a fellow. Your works are enough guarantee.

I have not yet received copies of *Homelife* nor have I received any honorarium. If the sum is small, I suggest that you give it to charity. But if the sum is fairly large, by all means send it to me so that next time I see you, we can eat *merienda*![9] You know, I have the deepest appreciation for your robustness of spirit, a sort of dynamism which is rare among writers.

Rick Demetillo

🍃 🍃 🍃

January 25, 1973

Dear Gilbert,

My last note to you was very brief. This time, I have some spare time to share with you.

Look at this new poem that I composed after supper last evening. I had seen a few days before old pictures of the American landing on the moon; and I thought, I could write a short poem about it. But I did not just want

---

[6] Professor Alejandrino G. Hufana, Demetillo's colleague at the University of the Philippines.

[7] U.P. Writers Workshop is one of the most prestigious writers' workshops in the Philippines, accepting only established writers to its summer program.

[8] Now known as The Silliman University National Writers Workshop, this institution is the oldest creative writing workshop in Asia. Founded by novelist Edilberto and his poet-wife Edith Tiempo, the workshop is patterned after the Iowa Writers Workshop. Their mentor, Paul Engle, long-time director of the Iowa Writers Workshop, encouraged and supported the couple.

[9] Snack.

another laudatory poem on the achievement, but try to relate it to the human condition and to man's failures in his dreams for justice, peace and love and faith. I also felt that the tone should not be overly optimistic, for the wickedness in man is a deadly, devious thing. Perhaps, I could end on a warning or the hint of it.

So, that is the genesis of this particular poem. I hope it will gladden you. It should fulfill your desire for substance, substance, substance.

I am having a time with trying to go about building a house. The GSIS[10] bureaucratic routine is fatiguing; and the decision to be made about whether we shall give it all to a contractor or administer the building by myself with only the labor to be contracted is giving me the willies. Prices are the very devil; they have gone up from last year's prices by as much as 40 percent. Imagine a poet doing all these things. But I need a house to house my family!

Since four days ago, I have been almost feverishly writing my City poems. At this rate, I should have a large manuscript before the year ends. When these poetic urges come, nothing, nothing can stop them from being written. Its a form of creative madness but one which I like. The writing of the novel takes a back seat.

Come any time you like to come. My house and my time are always open and available to my friends. By this time, you should know that.

I have revised, by the way, the cave poem and one or two others. My poems never get really finally finished. But it is good to revise as much as the work can bear it.

Goodbye for now, Gilbert. It's good to know that you are doing great in your activities, for it is God's will that we, his children, should be fully creative.

Affectionately your friend,
Rick Demetillo

---

[10] Government Service Insurance System, a pension fund.

February 10, 1973

Dear Gilbert,

I received your "pre-dieu" poem several days ago but had to wait for the weekend to write. I have been writing poetry incessantly for so many weeks now; and my thoughts go inward rather than focused to the outside world. I am sending you "Window Panes," which starts on something very mundane and ends with creative miracles and mystical light.

I hope you will like it.

I shall try to go to the Nolledo and Dimalanta[11] lectures, unless something very unexpected will come my way. Maybe, too, I shall be able to meet with you and your group. Sometime in the future, why don't we plan on a poetry recital, where some of the best poets in the country can read their poems?

> "when you were baptized by the birds and the bees
> under the shady pili nut"?

Maybe, lines like these should be weeded out of "ad primam." They are a little on the jolting side and may be re-worked to be more subtly ironic. But an image like "lizards are feasting on butterflies" has metaphysical insight and is good poetry.

The "ad vesperas" section seems the best of the sections, and the poetry is good.

I think at times that poetry makes extremely difficult demands on its practitioners. The intuition of which it is the form has to be respected; and that is involvement in perfection, which parallels the perfection of grace which saints live and experience.

The building of my house is going a good rate. The foundations have been laid. My architect-contractor says it will be a very strong house, though it's just small in size. It's going to have a large basement, where I can have a sort of studio, so the rest of the family will not disturb me. I hope also that the house will be good to look at.

---

[11] José Nolledo and Ofelia Dimalanta are respected Filipino poets.

I am going to send more poems to the United States and, maybe, arrange for the publication of a book. This depends on whether the editors there will find my work good enough to publish.

Write me once in a while. I always enjoy sharing from you and reading your poems or your stories. Good day now!

Rick Demetillo

P.S. Did I tell you that 18 years ago, I wrote "Sand and the Lolling City," based on a letter of Saint Cyprian to Donatus, a Roman convert? The city he was thinking of was Carthage, not far from Hippo, Saint Augustine's place and bishopric. Now, the setting has become Manila or Quezon City or any city anywhere! The spiritual conditions vary only very little.

🌿 🌿 🌿

February 15, 1973

Dear Gilbert,

Your last letter shows that you are undergoing an important crisis in your outward but, more so, in your inner life. Your decisions as to whether you should continue to study for an M.A. or a Ph.D. or Theology will affect your entire life; and I have passed my own such decisions to know that a misstep now will be of terrific effects on your entire life. I am praying for you, Gilbert, if prayers like mine can be of any help.

The question, ultimately, is what to do with your life? Do you want an academic success? Do you want a doctoral degree? Will that necessarily enrich your mind and your imagination so that taking it will be paramount? How true Frost's poem about "The roads diverged in a yellow wood."

I personally believe in your artistic life, that thing that makes you a special person. But you also have other gifts: moral sense (which now seems somewhat disturbed), possibly administrative talents. These gifts, in some persons, do not clash and need not clash. In my own case, I discovered that my Hamletic temperament prevents me from being an administrator or from being a businessman, even in academic matters. So, I shaped my life to just being the best teacher I can be plus being also a poet, how good I am not sure totally about. Given that decision, my life has ordered itself accordingly. It has given my life a simplicity and an orderliness which yields peace of mind, though at times, being human, I envy one or two people who have made successes of themselves in a more conventional way. But whenever I confront myself, I know that the course of my life was what was and is right for me.

We cannot make these decisions fully without the deep-searching which I am sure you are now undergoing. Pray to the good Lord to guide you and, having made a decision to stick to it and achieve inner peace.

I am deeply touched that my poetry has aroused deep stirrings in your mind and in your imagination. I can remember when Baudelaire, Yeats and others so moved me that I had to try to create works that could be, like theirs, at least, in intensity; and though, later, I wrote poetry that was different from theirs, at least, I had achieved a higher quality of perfection. Today, I try to achieve grace in the stylistic qualities, but also in grace in our sense of the word.

So, I think of you often these days, and hope that you will be led to the right decisions. The right decision is: that which will not violate your inner sense, so that you will feel the light of your inner life that will bless you and give you peace and contentment. But peace and contentment may not be the immediate state you will experience. We pursue one way and we think we will reach the end we seek, now, irreversibly; but you know as well as I do, that God has a way of leading us through a way we did not intend to follow, in the first place.

But, there, I sound like a very old man. You might even feel that there is a touch of senility in what I say!

The good God keep you, my friend.

Rick Demetillo

Saint Francis in Ecstasy
(To Gilbert Luis R. Centina III)

The saint emerges from a dark of caves
Made gentler by a trellis where the vine
Attest to life that sucks deep-rooted earth.
The figure has advanced on shoeless feet.
Against ascetic rocks, Saint Francis seems
Fragile as most created things are frail.

But sunlight is an aureole around his head;
Severe, the gown is softened by the sun.

What is man doing in this altitude?
The orb is shining, nimbus full of love,
Caressing field and houses with its warmth.
The trees burst into bloom and bear their fruits.

The worlds are vast, vast like an infinite;
But God can touch a man's heart with His love
This is God's poet praising day and night,
And all things: birds and beasts, the moss and weed.
See, there's a spring that bubbles from a rock.
It is the sluice of grace that nurtures earth.
The day has dappled all the hills with light
And led the saint to this ecstatic height.
The patient ass that waits to take its load,
Like men who work at industry or trade,
Crops at the succulent grass; a little bird
Seems listening to the poet's voice.
Love is the Good that we must celebrate.
See, all the verdurous boughs unfurl in love.
Above the hilltop, glory is a blaze,
And Brother Francis stands to chant his praise.

O living Light that subjugates the dark
And makes it serve the miracle of God,
Bless now your saint whose ecstasies are shared
By all who know the Sun and walk in love.

Ricaredo Demetillo

February 28, 1973

Dear Gilbert,

I am dedicating this poem of praise to our friendship. For me, it is the poem, since I wrote *La Via*, that I have returned in humility and faith to the fold of the Son, Lord of Light and Love, whom I celebrate.

If *La Via* was overcompensation, inviting hubris, this one poem, with all that will follow it, is restitution.

I am deeply grateful to you for many things. God keep you and do not lose your force of perception and grace.

The basic theme of *La Via*, I do not repudiate. But I have, on more mature premises, synthesized my religious and artistic presuppositions in a manner aligned to the larger, ore comprehensive vision which includes faith and love, as well as beauty, all attributes of God. Saint Francis, for me, is the great troubadour poet; and that's the reason I am using his figure in this poem of faith. I'll later on write you a longer letter.

Ricaredo Demetillo

March 3, 1973

Dear Gilbert,

I'm sorry I missed you when you came to the house. I look forward to another talk with you. In fact, sometime, I would like to visit with you at your galaxette, just to relate to your surroundings.

By this time, you should have received my last note with my poem on Saint Francis. Keep it. It is very important poem in both autobiographical-spiritual and artistic senses.

La Via, about which I wrote briefly to you, was premised on the presupposition that men's spiritual and creative fullness can be achieved to the fullest only in the proper exercise of their psycho-physical function, especially the sexual. Guilts, anxieties, and even madness result from an over-rigid denial of such functions. This premise I have not repudiated, though I have repudiated some beliefs regarding the Church and some beliefs and dogmas that do not seem to have any relevance for man. You will read it all in *La Via,* which some say is a *wicked* book, but to me a very important contribution to the values we live by as a people.

About my chief works in book form:
1. *No Certain Weather,* out of print, poems;
2. *La Via, A Spiritual Journey,* poems;
3. *Barter in Panay,* literary epic on justice and social cohesiveness;
4. *The Authentic Voice of Poetry,* criticism;
5. *Daedalus and Other Poems,* poems;
6. *Masks and Signature,* poems on the artists and their relevance to society;
7. *The Scare-Crow Christ,* the latest book to come out in a few weeks; poems.

All these works celebrate the interlocking themes that are really unique with me. I advise that they be studied in relation to one another. Except for *Daedalus, Masks and Signature,* and *The Scare-Crow Christ,* the others are out of print. There is a crying need for a complete edition of these poems!

The last book will be out in late March at the latest. I will furnish you with *The Diliman Review* special issue in which the poems appear. So with *Daedalus,* a small paperback. *Masks and Signature,* which can be ordered or bought from National Bookstore or from U.P. Press, costs ₱12.

You can borrow my personal copies of the out-of-print books. The Ateneo *Philippine Studies* contains long reviews of *Barter, La Via* (by [Emmanuel] Torres, and by a certain nun, who wrote very favorably on *Barter.*

When the City poems are completed, they should comprise my eighth book. I am sending you one of the poems, a very important addition to my vision of the contemporary world.

I sent the Saint Francis poem to *New Catholic World,* the address of which you sent. Let's hope it gets published there. Somehow, I feel it is the right magazine for the poem.

I am very glad that you have overcome your crisis. Life has many such, so don't be shocked at them. Also, since you have chosen the priesthood with its celibacy and all, you will have certain tensions, in respect to sexuality, your sexuality. You will need plenty of inner power to make possible a great sublimation, but I have the greatest confidence in your self and in your body to overcome this. Love a lot of people, create your poems and stories

(I don't think God wants you to give up either poetry or fiction, for if you have the gift, you will continue to write). Love and creativity are the best medicines; and I'm talking of love in its subliminal forms, at least for you.

See, I am writing you in a sort of bossing manner. Forgive me for that. But I'm talking common sense, a product of 53 years of experience and fumbling (with my own life)) and appalling mistakes. You now see a relaxed contented person. When I was younger, I was not so contented, nor was I very saintly or anything remotely like that! I have written of SIN in Book I of *La Via*. Book II deals with my search for a synthesis and a meaning out of the confusions that life can be, many, many times.

All along, though, I kept my integrity as a poet and as a person. Maybe, that's the reason I am still able to write; and I think now, that I'm still capable of writing some great poetry, maybe, my most mature and profound ones.

When my house will be completed and we can live in it, I'll have the honor and pleasure to invite you to bless it with your prayers. Not a ceremony, but just a prayer with my wife and me for hearers. I'm sure that God will bless the house and my family, with you. The prayers of a good priest are not to be taken lightly.

Sometimes, I smile to myself saying that you have been sent by God to me so that I my poetry will gain a new dimension.

My children are: Darnay, oldest 27, still single; Rebecca Linda, married, now Mrs. Pedro Abraham Jr., Lester and Weston, twins, still in college. Darnay is very gifted: I think he will make a very good painter and sculptor, if he pushes himself.

Thank you for Saint Augustine's thoughts. *Masks* contains a long poem about him. He is one of the mountains that define one's consciousness; a terrific psychologist, a guilt-love-driven man. I believe I understand him.

Come to the house during the weekend, so I will be around.

God bless and keep you, my little Augustinian priest!

Rick Demetillo

❧ ❧ ❧

3-3-73

Dear Gilbert,

   We must speak to our generation in contemporary terms. This is the latest in the City poems.

Business Executive

    Day in, day out, in bright committee rooms,
    With weighty tables and straight-backed chairs,
    With others like himself, all important men,
    He talks and tersely gestures—policies.

    Business and power that business represents
    Engross his thoughts, as they must, when
    Ambition prods the proud executive.
    His juniors make obsequious bows to him.
    Decisions must be geared to what expands
    The business empire which he represents.
    Rapacity, even in the best of men,
    Is in the clipped assurance of his words.
    How else can business power be maintained?
    How else can Gain be planned and organized?
    An era of the most advanced techniques
    Has shaped this man, as whirlpools shape a stone.

    So in a time when persons seem abstract
    That they can be ignored or used as pawns,
    This tycoon rides rough-shod over sentiments.
    Power is ruthless like any Genghis Khan.

    But still he feels a gnawing discontent.
    The functionary feels he is less a man.
    An ulcer is a nagging in his guts.
    There is an insipid taste in many things.

He drives a Cadillac to and back from work.
Only the best he orders in food and drink.
The sleek face shows a boundless confidence;
But still there is the tell-tale clue of *Angst*.
One night, he dreams he slips upon the stairs
And wakes up, silly, that it is all a dream.
In still another night, he is amazed to see
That he has for a heart, a dried-up hole.

Ricaredo Demetillo

🌿 🌿 🌿

3-23-73

Dear Gilbert,

Here's Osei-san for a change. I have always thought Rizal's Japanese sweetheart was romantic and could be used for a drama or a poem. It's only today that my meditations on her have crystallized into this sad monologue. I have put into it memories and thoughts of women loved and lost. The patriotic element is minimal in the work.

I spoke on my works, by the way, at Adamson University. The audience was very appreciative; some very enthusiastic. I discovered that many may have studied my poems. I read "Rebellious Sonnets" and "Business Executive," but having no more time, I failed to read "Saint Francis." Professor Bendero's class surprised me with a gift—a pair of cuff links and a tie pin! That was very kind and thoughtful of them!

Darnay designed the cover of *The Scare-Crow Christ*, a bend laborer with a spade in black and the name of the book and mine done in green. The magazine copies should be out by month's end; the hardcover copies may come out a little later, for the binding and the cover work take longer to do. I'm grateful to *The Diliman Review* for the special issue!

My two essays on San Juan as critic and my observations on artists are in the latest issues of *Solidarity*. You may wish to read them, especially the San Juan piece, for it is my answer to Marxist criticism on literature.

I wish later on to gather my essays for another volume. I have a lot of various critiques lying around! Some of them are, I think, important utterances on the philosophic implications of art and literature.

Thank you ever so much for your friendship. It has crystallized many things in my creative life.

When ideas of new poems congeal to final form, I'll write you a longer letter. I seem to have arrived at one of my highest creative tasks. Best to exploit this.

By the way—is it true that [our friend] is confined at Saint Luke's Psychiatric Ward? This may only be rumor. I do hope so, for he is also a good friend and fellow poet.

Rick Demetillo

P.S. I have been sick for a few days, feeling very weak, the weakness caused by an old ailment. But I managed to write "Osei-san" and "Kapinangan in Exile," both monologues. I might try a whole verse play, especially on the latter subject.

Your poem, short as it is, seems quite fine. Try to work towards allusive clarity—a thing Filipino poets seem to find hard to accomplish. We are sadly given to rococo and baroque circumlocutions. I try to fight that tendency in my own work.

My long, long short story, "Journey Into the Mist," is with Sionil José,[12] also my "Mirrors of Perseus." I don't know whether the story will be published. If so, I will be hugely happy. Did I tell you that I'm writing a novel?

I will revise the City poems in time for the Cultural Center poetry contest! Wish me luck!

R.D.

---

[12] F. Sionil José, a National Artist of the Philippines for Literature, was a well-known novelist and publisher of *Solidarity*, a respected literary journal, now defunct.

❦ ❦ ❦

April 5, 1973

Dear Gilbert,

I am writing you to say that the Sumakwel and Kapinangan tragedy is finished, typed, and all set for anything. I feel rather triumphant about this, for I know it is one of my biggest creative achievements. The entire action is supposed to last just a few days to achieve unity of plot, time and action. My characters are really heroic, all the three of them; but I have used tension and irony to add density to them. This is a long play; the whole action, including changes of scenery and such, will last two hours or so. Now that the typing is done, I feel rather tired, but in a nice way. I'll take it easy for a while and not write at all.

Your decision to study at Ateneo is a very good one. As you say, they are somewhat more human and humane at Ateneo. Their English department is rather good, and I am sure you are just the type that would benefit from their program. Rolando Tinio[13] is a good, creative teacher and director. Torres[14] is a fairly interesting poet...Father de la Costa[15] is quite reputable, but he will not be in your line of training. Maybe, some American teachers there are also teachers with some sparks in them....

The hardcover part of my new book is still being done and may take a little more time than the magazine issue. I hope I can have the copies before the end of the month. I shall be glad to be part of a poetry reading session to help the sales of *The Scare-Crow Christ*.

I am glad you like those poems in *Daedalus*. Your choices seem almost infallible. "There Is a Part of Me Born on Some Battlefield" is a very early poem done just after the War. "Tragic Victory" was chosen by Viray[16] for

---

[13] Poet and dramatist Rolando Tinio was later proclaimed National Artist of the Philippines for Theater and Literature.
[14] Award-winning poet Emmanuel Torres.
[15] Father Horacio de la Costa, SJ, a Filipino historian.
[16] Noted poet Manuel E. Viray was the editor of *Heart of the Island: An Anthology of Philippine Poetry in English* in three editions. The first came out in 1947.

his anthologies. My new book has a lot of these shorter poems: some are very meaty, I like to think. *Masks* is basically meditational, central to which is grace, both in the artistic and the religious sense.

I am glad that you have an early vacation. You can use that reading a lot or doing some of your writing. The important thing is that you are gaining new and deeper experiences and that you are improving your craft to project these experiences. You are the type who profits from all possible experiences, including the unpleasant ones. The latter are necessary as the happier ones to add dimensions to your thoughts. I hope you will be equal to the crises that happen in your life. Some of us writers pay for such crises that happen in your life. Pray to God you won't undergo that calvary.

The good Lord keep you and bless your work.

Rick Demetillo

🍃 🍃 🍃

U.P. Infirmary
University of the Philippines
June 9, 1973

Dear Gilbert,

I am writing this from a hospital bed. Tomorrow I shall have a series of X-rays, both for kidneys and lungs; an ailment or ailments of a serious nature are sapping my energies and burning the fuel of my body, and the doctors are worried, as I am, about what's burning me. My weight has gone down very low - 16 lbs.!

I have been wondering why you have not come to visit as you wrote you would. In fact, I was expecting you on June 2 and 3, so we could talk. Are you busy with new plans; enrollment, new responsibilities? At any rate, you owe me a long talk at least or a long letter to compensate! Comfort for a sick man!

For several weeks I did not do any writing. But three days ago, I did a splendid meditation: "Poet at Angkor Wat," in unrhymed hexameters. Who has not read of Angkor Wat? I've meditated on its significance for quite a while and this 3-page poem is the evocation of the religious faith, the proud ambitions and the ultimate decline and death, the last symbolized by the crumbling of the rocks at Angkor and their being swallowed by wild forests, until rediscovered to the amazed eyes of the tourists and archaeologists. Tragedy—that's what it is; the human adventure vaulting to a peak, then plunging to obscurity. Jayavarman VII's drive to religious zeal by leprosy, impoverished his land with his feverish conquests and megalomaniac building, and maintenance of great religious sanctuaries, such as Angkor Thom. A strange great man!

Dr. Gémino Abad will soon come out with a very fine book. It really pays to have culture at the service of the creative imagination. I personally welcome every artistic contribution to national culture.

I have met your brother, the one who is at Ateneo, and enjoyed chatting with him for a while. Thanks for your comments on *The Scare-Crow Christ*!

Good day and the good Lord keep you!

Rick Demetillo

🍃 🍃 🍃

July 26, 1973

My dear Gilbert,

Thank you very much for your letter, which I received only this morning. I am glad to know that *Homelife* is publishing my two poems. What are they?

I am glad that you find *La Via* challenging and really not heretical. I mistrust, of course, the idea that I am a mystic of sorts, though there have been certain experiences of mine that appear somewhat strange, and to my rational mind, a little baffling. I say mistrust for in such matters, God can easily become Devil, and complacency can result from such experiences that are out of the usual. To go into the depths can be courting disaster, even to the point of becoming incense. Yet, of course, one must meet that risk, for how can one achieve profundity except by diving into the depths of life?

I am planning on, at least, two more dramas, one on the subject of "The Cripples," projecting the spiritual predicament of men and women today, who cannot find joy and grace because they lack the capacity to love: others, themselves, and God. Until that love becomes a light that warms one's life, one is alienated from himself. The other subject I wish to write on and about which I mull a lot nowadays is that of Mary Magdalene, who had seven devils cast out of her by Jesus. But I wish to make Mary Magdalene a Filipina, living in our present time, grimly dissatisfied by her grasping at all the sensuous-sensual aspects of modern life. Maybe, I am a bit obsessed by this subject, as Dostoevsky was, for it hits a central predicament in modern life. Pray that I will be able to create something out of the usual in this regard.

> Jesus, my Saviour, look on me
> For I am weary and opprest.
> I come to cast myself on Thee.

These fragments of a hymn has been running a little mouse in my head all morning. I am planning to use it in "The Cripples," for it has a great power of suggestibility. The sooner I work on these plots the better, for I want to go back to the rest of my epic.

...Behn Cervantes[17] has wonderful news about my drama. He said to me yesterday that the play is very good, for everything is visualized (theme, characterization, etc.) and that it is "very definitely" actable. He also said that the language is elevated, really something parallel to Greek and Shakespearean dramas, and will need really good actors, who can do justice to the language. I am seeking Mr. Rolando Tinio, too, today at Ateneo to get his verdict. I need to negotiate with our Presidential Committee on Culture at U.P. to have my play produced. This is full production, if at all, and may need an allocation big enough to take care of costumes and scene sets.

About experiments in language: there is need to do these intricate verbal play early in one's career as a poet, to enable one to achieve flexibility. Shakespeare has a euphuist phase, in his early works, where there is a lot of word play, but later, he could create marvelous clear effects, rich, however, in levels of meaning because he had mastered the language. The style which is clear can be achieved only after a long arduous discipline. [Poet Federico Licsi] Espino may graduate into that later on...if he does not get diverted to too much criticism. I still feel that he is relatively minor in his achieve-

---

[17] Critically-acclaimed film and stage director Behn Cervantes made quality Filipino films in the 1970s.

ments so far; and I hope the big things will come in the future; how near or far, we cannot determine.

I hope for your poetry this clarity, this unity, and the grace, wedded to tensile strength, which is the hallmark of the greatest poems. In my case, the experiments go on, for I know that at my age, I can accomplish more miracles of creativity. In the matter of control, *The Heart of Emptiness Is Black* is probably superior to *La Via*, although *La Via* had a power that, rough in places, could dredge up significant insights.

I have a new set of four copies of the drama, typed by my friend, Mrs. Gutierrez. That makes a total of eight copies. Maybe, I can lend you a copy soon so you will have a chance to read this work. [Nick] Joaquin's play is baroque performance, mine is really classic.

I want to write more short lyrics after I put aside these demands on the larger projects. In fact, I have been playing around with ideas about a poem based on our visit to San Agustín in Intramuros. Ditto with the Civilizers. You Augustinians have shaped the spiritual life of the world a lot. That should challenge you young novices to plan on more achievements of a comparable *quality*....

I am reading that big sensual volume of *The Golden Legend* by Father Jacobus de Voragine, who was kind of abbot in the Catholic Middle Ages.[18] It's really a big *Lives of the Saints*. That's how I got interested in Mary Magdalene and in Saint Augustine. Much of the book deals with the miracles in the lives of these exemplary persons and evoke the quaint beliefs of that period; but some really contain wonderful insights. Friedrich Heer's searching volume on *The Intellectual History of Europe* is also on my desk. My somewhat provincial view of European intellectual history is receiving a wider point of view; am fascinated by Erasmus, for instance, or Paracelsus and Jacob Boehme.

...Do come and visit soon. It's always a pleasure to talk to you. And write.

Rick Demetillo

---

[18] De Voragine (born circa 1228, died 1298) was a chronicler and archbishop of Genoa.

Friday, Aug. 24, 1973

Dear Gilbert,

You have been on my mind since the other day when you came. I hope that you decide your future on that prospect which will best fulfill what you desire deepest in your self. I gave you certain options and possibilities and your decision, I trust, will be in order to best fulfill your spiritual quest.

About the possibility of teaching this summer at San Agustín[19] in Iloilo. If the summer session will last for six weeks, I shall charge San Agustín about 1600 pesos, which will be the equivalent to my salary at U.P. for the period, and an additional fee of 200 pesos for transportation, via air. My offhand remark last time was on the spur of the moment, equivalent to an honorarium here to teach a course during summer term. Going to Iloilo and staying there for 6 weeks will entail more expense, I am positive. But I shall be happy to go on the war path, if my conditions are met.

...Pray for me, dear Gilbert. I've never fully realized how deeply committed I am to Christian values until I sat down to collect my thoughts for the speech [for a religious convention].

I am praying for you, Gilbert. Where you will serve as layman or priest, I am sure that your life is in the hands of God. To reach him often is to walk certain detours, but the final destination is the same.

Yours in grace,
Rick Demetillo

September 13, 1973

My dear Gilbert,

I am a little dazzled by this poem, which I enclose. It is the last of the almost hundred poems that I have written in the last *seven* days, a celebration of the Redeemed Life, based on the archetype of Lazarus in the New Testament. I am tentatively naming this new book of poems *I, Lazarus, Troubadour*, assuming that he whom Jesus raised from the dead was and is a poet, celebrating his chance to live a second life.

---

[19] University of San Agustín, the first university in Western Visayas in the Philippines and the only Augustinian university in the Asia-Pacific region.

Sometimes I almost want to cry, because of these seizures of creativity. The last this happened was with *La Via*, in 1958. My long works have been done without this illuminating ecstasy, for instance, *The Heart of Emptiness Is Black*. In contrast to *La Via*, which contains rebellious attacks on the Church and on religious people, this one is entirely lyric affirmation and evocation, the purest songs that have come to birth through my hands. Also, the line schemes are most varied and highly interesting. Usually, my basic form is iambic pentameter, but this time, there are many unusual variations.

Do you believe that there are a few men seized by God? I believe that implicitly. The whole world is transfigured by this experience of Light.

The "Hail, Mary" poem was done half an hour ago. Before that I was reading from Luke's Gospel, the first few chapters and of a sudden, I began taking notes about some lines that struck me especially lovely and meaningful; and out of these I created the poem; only, I was afraid that I might introduce some indelicacies which would repel some sensibilities, in the treatment of what is traditionally holy. I had to do a most delicate creation of a pure song: Catholic, as you would say. Anyway, I am sending you the carbon copy of this miraculous thing. I think that is holy.

I will type several copies of *Lazarus, Troubadour*, so I can have it prepared for publication. I wish San Agustín[20] has plenty of money to publish a work like this, which is to me a gift of the Mysterious. It is approximately one hundred twenty pages long; and if it should be published by whatever agency, I wish to have it done on exceptionally beautiful paper and covered in really good cloth, with jacket.

Maybe, you can fetch me to go to San Agustín[21] by next Sunday, September 23. I would like to be there when you celebrate Mass. I am very serious Gilbert, for between us, you have given me greater insight into my own relationship to the Church, especially to Christ our Lord.

Our good, loving Father keep you for His purpose.

Yours in deep friendship,
Rick Demetillo

---

[20] Order of Saint Augustine.
[21] Our Lady of Grace Parish in Guadalupe, Makati City, where the Augustinians used to maintain a seminary for their theology students, including the author.

October 25, 1973

My dear Gilbert,

I have been enjoying your letter last. Your remarks about the *PIC*[22] writers have amused me, and I must say most of what you say is right. [A poet we both know] has a streak of the grotesque about him and what he writes; perhaps, that is a symptom of sickness, for I heard that he broke down at Iowa and may not have gotten out of his troubles as yet. Those take time to really heal and to be sorted out. But he is on his way out of his spiritual calvary, which every writer, if he must amount to something, will have to undergo. That is why my archetypal symbol of the artistic activity is almost always in the form of search, a journey that involves great difficulties. The labyrinth is part of this journey, too, and as often as not, one gets lost trying to get out of the dreadful mystification of that labyrinthine passage. *La Via*, in the hell and purgatory sections, are full of that type of symbolism, for the writer is engaged in the effort to get out, desperate at times.

I think that our best friends and acquaintances among the writers are engaged in that search, that way out. So, be not too harsh on them, for they might succeed, with God's grace, to get out and to fulfill the highest promises of their gifts. Espino[23] interests me much in this regard.

Today, I have been given another ecstatic seizure, a kind of coda to the lyric music of the Troubadour poems, to which the poems rightly belong. I just came back, an hour ago, from Mrs. [Fern] Grant's house, where I delivered the new batch of ten new poems, the most profound in a number of ways of these outpourings. Mrs. Grant is the publisher [of New Day Publishers] for the United Church of Christ in the Philippines; and she has accepted the whole manuscript for an early publication date. My Protestant brethren are beginning to take me seriously as poet-seer or something and I am happy for that fact.

I think that the fact that your fellow seminarians read my poems proves the catholicity of true poetry. One should be read for the universal truth and the beauty of one's works, not whether he belongs to a sect or what.

---

[22] A men's magazine published in Manila in the 1970s.
[23] Award-winning Filipino poet Federico Licsi Espino Jr.

My poems are in loving search for their readers and lovers, and I expect more and more people will find in them the patent for their spiritual strivings, for there are many people all over the world, who are looking for release from their striving and their agony of soul. As our Saint Augustine says, the heart is restless until it rests in God. I do not care to be less than catholic in my appeal.

I also wrote another letter to Engle[24] and enclosed the new sheaf that I wrote today. I told him that I'm interested in an American edition of the Troubadour poems....

Do you notice that in the Troubadour poems, the style is stripped of almost all adjectives? That's because I wish to show man (Lazarus) bare of all extraneous elements as he stands before the Lord of Light, God. This style is as simple and as dignified and direct as possible: no involved sentences, no pretentious language. God should see man totally naked, as he must, of course.

You know, my friend, that I value very much your regard for me and the poems I write. It is humbling to know that we have formed our relationship in this satisfying way. My spiritual awareness has deepened much since our friendship started. And I am aware that your own self has progressed a lot, too, since your knowing me.

...I am preparing and finishing the almost finished work: the drama and the City poems. When I am through with these, I shall go back to the novel. I think I know exactly how to go about writing this long work. It may really become a series of shorter works, but all about the person who gradually discovers and finds the way to his highest self. Nothing is more difficult or more distasteful to most people than to ask them to discover their true selves. Herman Hesse, the Nobel Prize novelist, has done things that approximate the same general experiences....

Your friend,
Rick Demetillo

---

[24] Paul Engle, then director of the Iowa Writers Workshop.

GLOSSARY

A

Aetas - The original inhabitants of the Philippines who now live in isolated mountain areas. They were driven from the lowlands by the Austronesian migrations, which came before the arrival of the Spaniards. 58, 60, 62.
Anitos - The spirits or deities worshiped by Philippine natives before the coming of the Spaniards in the sixteenth century. 1, 58, 63.
Ati-atihan Festival - An annual religious celebration in the town of Kalibo in the central Philippine province of Aklan in honor of the Child Jesus. Of animist origin, the festival of thanksgiving, highlighted by Mardi-gras style street dancing and procession, was appropriated by Spanish religious missionaries who added Christian elements. 97.

B

Babaylan - A religious leader in the pre-Spanish Philippines who acted as a seer, priestess/shaman, and faith healer. The term especially applied to herbalists in the Visayas. 62.
Baguio - The summer capital of the Philippines developed by the Americans in the early part of the twentieth century. It enjoys fantastic weather all year long and is popular with local and foreign tourists. 34, 97.
Bathala - The creator of the universe or chief deity, according to the belief of early Filipinos. 1.
Barkada - A gang or group of friends. 97.

C

Carabaos - Water buffaloes. 53, 83.
Chongos- Filipino slang for monkeys. 80.
Conquistadores - The Spanish term refers to military leaders who conquered new territories in the Philippines and South America in the name of the Spanish monarch beginning in the fifteenth century. 37, 83.
Cultural Center of the Philippines - Built by former Philippine First Lady Imelda Romualdez Marcos, the building has been the preferred venue for most, if not all, of the country's major arts and culture events since its inauguration in 1969. 2, 124.

D

Datus - Tribal chieftains in the pre-Spanish Philippines. 56, 57, 60.
Don(s) - Of Spanish origin, the term is an honorific used to convey respect when used before a man's name or *doña* when used before a woman's name. 6, 14, 83.

E

Ermita - Manila's tourist district. 106.
Estero - A drainage canal. 94, 104.

F

Fort Santiago - A Spanish fort guarding the walled city of Intramuros in Manila, which the Spaniards founded in 1571. 106.
Frailes - Friars. 79.

H

Hidalgos - Spanish for gentlemen. 83.
Hiligaynon - A Philippine language spoken in Western Visayas. 87, 94, 135.

I

Indios - The term used by Spanish colonizers to describe native inhabitants of the Philippines and their other colonies in Ibero America. 80.
Intramuros - Adelantado Miguel López de Legazpi founded the walled city of Intramuros in 1571. From this original settlement, Manila evolved into the country's most important city as the seat of government. 82, 154.

J

Jeepneys - The Philippines' primary mode of public transport. Abandoned by the U.S. Army after the Second World War ended in the Philippines, the military jeeps were converted by Filipinos into colorful vehicles to ferry passengers, becoming a ubiquitous and unique national symbol of ingenuity. 54.

K

Kaingin - A clearing, usually in mountainous areas, used for agriculture by slash-and-burn farmers. This destructive practice is blamed for forest denudation. 82.
Kalachuchi - A flowering plant known as plumeria in other places. It is native to the Caribbean, Mexico, the Cook Islands, and Brazil. 106.

L

Maharlika - Men belonging to the feudal warrior class on the island of Luzon before the Christianization of the Philippines. 57.
Mindanao - The third largest island of the Philippine archipelago, hailed as the "land of promise" by Christian settlers. It is home to a restive Muslim population. 98.

N

Naric - It stands for the defunct National Rice and Corn Corporation, which sold government-subsidized cheap rice and corn in the Philippines. 34.

Glossary

Nipa - In the Philippines, it refers to the nipa palm leaves, mainly used for thatch roofing in poor areas. A house with such roofing is called by locals a nipa hut, which is usually associated with the poor. 83, 136.

P

Pasig River - A 15.5-mile river divides Manila into its northern and southern halves. It connects Laguna de Bay to Manila Bay. 53.

Pagsanjan - A resort town south of Manila famous for its waterfalls. 97.

Q

Quiapo - A Manila district known for its Church of the Black Nazarene, which attracts millions of devotees to its annual feast day, and for Plaza Miranda, Manila's equivalent of New York's Union Square or London's Hyde Park. 106.

Quinta Market - One of Manila's busiest public markets. 106.

S

San Agustín Church - The oldest existing stone church building in the Philippines. Situated in Intramuros, Manila, the Augustinians built it. From this church, the Christianization of the Philippines was plotted for centuries until Eastern and Western cultures were fused, giving the Southeast Asian nation its unique identity. 2, 113, 124.

T

Tondo - A notorious slum district in Manila. 106.

Toro - An actual sex performance between a man and a woman in front of a paying audience. 106.

INDEX

A

Abad, Gémino H. IX, 148
Abia Polvorosa, Father Santos, OSA X
Adam 2, 17, 38, 45, 46, 65, 120
Adamson University. 144
Aetas 58, 60, 61, 155
Agape 26, 37, 38, 42, 47, 124, 125
Aguirre, Antonio X
Aguirre, Marimar X
Alcibiades and Socrates 26
Alegre, Edilberto N. XIV
Alfon, Estrella D. X
Alpha, and Omega 84
Álvarez, Father Jerónimo, OSA XI
America II, XV, 79, 155, 156
American XIV, 35, 85, 106, 127, 128, 134, 146, 154
Angkor Thom 105, 148
Angkor Wat 104, 105, 147
anitos 1, 58, 62, 155
Aportadera, Dean Teresita X
arbolario 65
Arboleda, Father Andres R. Jr., SSP X
Arcellana, Francisco 121
archetypal symbol 82, 122, 125, 126, 153
archetype 3, 112, 151
Arguilla, Manuel 80
Arnold, Matthew 24
Arreza Milan, Father Rodolfo X
art II, VI, XVII, 6, 66, 70, 75, 76, 97, 124, 129
art is Calvary II, XVII, 97, 124
  Calvary II, XVII, 97, 124
artist II, X, XI, XVI, XVII, 6, 65, 66, 68, 69, 70, 75, 77, 78, 79, 81, 82, 83, 84, 92, 97, 98, 124, 125
artist is Proteus 68
Ateneo 7, 141, 146, 148, 149
Ateneo de Manila University 7
Ati-atihan Festival 155
Auden XV, 75
Augustinian III, IX, X, XI, XIII, 2, 105, 111, 112, 122, 127, 128, 142
Avanceña, Nenita X
Avestruz Salcedon, Father Lester X

B

babaylan 155
Bang-gotbanwa 58
Banggot-banwa 58, 61, 62
barkada 95, 155

Barter in Panay VI, XV, 1, 4, 5, 7, 31, 56, 59, 61, 63, 127, 141
Basque IX, X
Bathala 1, 155
Baudelaire XV, 26, 72, 138
Bernardo, Constancio 80
Bishop Emeritus of Iquitos IX
Blackmur, Richard XIV
Blake 73, 113
Blessed Virgin Mary 118
Boddhisatva 25
Boehme, Jacob 150
Botticelli 74
Budapest 23, 24
Buddha 23, 24, 94
Bulfinch, Thomas 26
Bulosan, Carlos 79
Burke, Kenneth XIV

C

Cabalquinto, Luis X
Cadmus 25
Calvary 89, 120
Calypsos of doubt 44
Campos, Father Pietro, SSP X
canvas 78, 81
carabaos 52, 80, 81, 155
Carbonell, Rolando 127
Carthage 28, 29, 137
Carunungan, Celso Al. X
Casper, Leonard 7
Catholic XIII, 4, 74, 100, 119, 128, 141, 150, 152
Catholic Spain 74
Centina III, Gilbert Luis R. II, XVII, 2, 3, 7, 68, 70, 99, 107, 112, 115, 119, 131, 138
Centina, Louella Cecilia R. 7
Centina, Romeo R. XI
Centiramo Publishing II, 99
Central Philippines College XIV
Cervantes 74, 149
Chavet Rodríguez, Robert 81
chongos 155
Christ II, VI, XV, XVII, 1, 2, 3, 4, 5, 10, 11, 12, 13, 14, 17, 27, 36, 42, 43, 44, 54, 73, 74, 76, 77, 80, 83, 84, 85, 86, 88, 91, 94, 95, 96, 97, 98, 99, 107, 108, 114, 117, 118, 120, 121, 122, 124, 125, 127, 130, 131, 141, 144, 146, 148, 152, 153
Christian XIII, 1, 2, 4, 5, 13, 20, 26, 27, 33, 35, 52, 107, 108, 116, 128, 151, 155, 156
Christianity 28, 100, 116
Christianization 156, 157
Christian morality XIII, 5
church XIII, XIV, XVII, 1, 2, 3, 6, 19, 20, 23, 33, 34, 38, 39, 41, 42, 54, 97, 100, 109, 111,

112, 116, 122, 123, 124, 125, 130, 140, 152, 153, 157
Circean lore 69
Circes 44
city of God 2, 107, 108, 109
city of man 2, 101, 102, 103, 104, 107, 108, 111, 121, 125
clericalism XIII, 99
Colcol & Co. Publishing XI
Colegio San Agustín Makati XI
Columbus 34, 66
conquistadores 37, 81
Creator 1, 3, 5, 6, 26, 44, 52, 73, 84, 108, 120, 122, 126
Cuadra, Jolico 7
Cuadra, Marcelina X
Cultural Center of the Philippines 2, 122, 155

D

Daedalus XV, 1, 4, 5, 31, 48, 49, 52, 55, 127, 141, 146
Daedalus and Other Poems 1, 4, 5, 31, 48, 55, 63, 127, 141
Dante XV, 31, 32
datus 57, 59
Datus 155
Daumier 75
David-Maramba, Asuncion 43
De la Costa, Father Horacio, SJ 146
Delacroix 74
De Linaje, José María Alonso Alonso X
Demetillo, Ricaredo
  Demetillo I, II, VII, XIII, XIV, XVI, 1, 2, 3, 5, 7, 8, 20, 31, 48, 56, 60, 64, 65, 68, 69, 70, 76, 100, 101, 107, 119, 123, 129, 130, 131, 132, 133, 134, 135, 136, 137, 138, 139, 140, 141, 142, 143, 144, 145, 146, 147, 148, 149, 150, 151, 152, 153, 154
De Miguel, María Ana Romo X
demiurge 66
Deriada, Leoncio P. X
De Urdaneta, Fray Andrés, OSA IX, 105
Diez, Father Regino, OSA XI
Dimalanta, Ofelia 136
Divina Commedia 31, 40
Dominican 77
Donatus 28, 29, 137
Don Carlos Palanca Memorial Awards 6
Dostoevsky 69, 76, 149
Dumaguete City XIV
Dumangas XIV

E

Echeverría, Fray Nicolás, OSA XI
Eden 38, 63

El Greco 69
Eliot, T. S. 36
Engle, Paul XIV, 30, 134, 154
Epimetheus 26
Erasmus 150
Ermita 104, 156
Eros 26, 30, 37, 38, 42, 47, 111, 124, 125
Espino, Federico Licsi Jr. X, 26, 56, 132, 153
Estember, John Peter X
estero 92, 156
Eucharist 11, 116
Europe 25, 54, 79, 150
Ezcurra, Santiago P., OSA XI

F

Fernandez, Doreen G. XIV
Ferrer Cruz, Father Pedro X
First Cause 52
Florentino, Alberto S. X
Fort Santiago 104, 156
frailes 77, 156
Freud 75, 76

G

Gabriel 43
Gamalinda, Eric X
García Centeno, Bishop Julián, OSA
García, Father Quentín , OP XI
Garcia Villa, José XVI, 69, 80, 113
Gauguin 72
Gernale, Roger X
Gide, André 76
Girum 58
God II, V, VI, IX, XVII, 2, 3, 6, 7, 11, 12, 13, 14, 15, 16, 17, 18, 20, 21, 22, 29, 43, 44, 46, 52, 53, 55, 59, 61, 63, 66, 73, 76, 77, 80, 82, 83, 84, 87, 90, 97, 98, 99, 105, 107, 108, 109, 110, 111, 112, 113, 114, 115, 116, 118, 119, 120, 121, 122, 123, 124, 125, 126, 128, 135, 138, 139, 140, 142, 147, 148, 151, 152, 153, 154
Goethe's Faust 31
Golden Jubilee Award for Poetry 6
Gómez Rivera, Guillermo X
González, N.V.M 80
Gospel 22, 107, 119, 152
Greece VI, 25
Greek and Shakespearean dramas 149
Greek concept of love 26, 30
Grupo de Oración X
Gurong-gurong 59, 60, 61, 62

H

Hadji Mustafa 23, 24
Hawthorne 75

Index

Heer, Friedrich 150
Heliconian pride 25
Herr Otto 23, 24
Hesse, Herman 154
hidalgos 156
Hiligaynon 85, 91, 132, 156
Hinaktakan Beach 55
Hippolita and Delphine 26
Hokusai, Ghwashiki 74
Homais 75
Homelife 129, 131, 134, 148
Homer XV, 31, 75
Hosillos, Lucila X
hubris 49
Hufana, Alejandrino G. IX, 134
humanism XIII, 5
Humanities 76, 129

I

Iglesía del Carmen IX, X, XVII
Iloilo XIV, 151
Index Librorum Prohibitorum 100
Indiana State University XIV
indios 156
Intramuros 80, 150, 156, 157
Iowa State University 30
Iowa Writers Workshop XIV, 134, 154
Italy 25

J

Jacobus de Voragine 150
Jalandoni, Magdalena G. 91
Japanese 105, 144
Jáuregui, Vicente II, X
Jayavarman VII 105, 148
jeepney 94
Jesus Christ 11, 14, 108, 118
    11, 14, 108, 118
Joaquin, Nick 59, 80, 129
José Rizal Centennial Award 6
Jota, Jenny X

K

Kafka 76
kaingin 156
kalachuchi 104
Kapinangan 59, 60, 62, 145, 146
Kierkegaard 76
King City XI
Knight of Columbus 34
Kuryosai 74

L

Lady Murasaki 74
La Via VI, XVI, 1, 2, 3, 4, 5, 6, 7, 31, 32, 33, 38,
    39, 40, 41, 42, 43, 48, 109, 110, 112, 115,
    119, 127, 140, 141, 142, 148, 150, 152,
    153
La Via: A Spiritual Journey XVI, 1, 4, 5, 6, 31, 40,
    41, 63, 127
Lazarus VII, XIII, 1, 3, 4, 5, 6, 7, 11, 19, 20, 83, 99,
    100, 112, 113, 114, 115, 116, 117, 118,
    120, 121, 122, 125, 126, 127, 129, 151,
    152, 154
Lazarus, Troubadour VII, XIII, 1, 3, 4, 5, 6, 7, 19,
    20, 100, 112, 115, 116, 120, 121, 127,
    151, 152
Letter of Ricaredo Demetillo 2, 3, 68, 70, 107, 119
Lin Po 74
Liquete, Father Gregorio, OSA XI
literature X, XIV, XVII, 4, 5, 76, 144
liturgy and worship 100
Longinus 12, 13
López, Father Rafael XI
Lowell, Robert XIV, 30
Lucifer 120, 122
Luna, Juan 78
Lutheran reform III
Luther, Martin III

M

Madaket 23
Magasaysay-Ho, Anita 80
Magdalene 43, 118, 119, 121, 148, 149, 150
maggots of fear VI, 22
Magno, C. Meng 7
maharlika 57, 156
Makatunaw 56, 57
Manansala, Vicente 80
Manila XI, XIV, XV, 2, 7, 23, 26, 28, 43, 54, 91,
    101, 104, 127, 128, 137, 153, 156, 157
Marcos, Ferdinand E. 132, 133
Marikudo 58, 61
Mariscal, Lauro Rodríguez, OSA IX
Marquez, Fred M. X
martial law XVI, 132, 133
Martin, Father General Nolan, OSA XI
Marylake Shrine of Our Lady of Grace XI
Masks and Signature VI, 1, 2, 4, 5, 7, 64, 67, 69, 70,
    72, 74, 75, 76, 80, 81, 82, 127, 141
Matthew 14
Melville, Herman 31, 75
Merton, Thomas 26
Michaelangelo 69
Mindanao 95, 156
Moby Dick 31

Modigliani 72
Moral Antón, Father Alejandro, OSA XI
Moses 14
Mother Ambrosia X
mountebank 65, 71
Muzones, Ramon L. 91

N

Naric. See National Rice and Corn Admnistration 34, 156
National Library of the Philippines IX
Navales, Estrella X
Neguri X, XVII
Nereid 68
New Criticism XV, 129
New Society 133
New Testament 2, 3, 112, 151
New York II, 4, 26, 81, 99, 100, 127, 128, 157
Nieto, Father Marcelino XI
nipa 157
Nobel Prize 154
No Certain Weather V, 1, 4, 5, 8, 17, 24, 30, 127, 141
Nolan, Father Martin , OSA XI
Nolledo, José 136
Norada, Conrado J. 91
North Africa 28
North Star 44

O

Ocampo, Hernando 81, 82
Oedipus and Jocasta 26
Orcasitas, Father Miguel Ángel, OSA XI
Orthodox 100
Osei-san 105, 106, 144, 145
Our Hidden Galaxette IV, XI

P

Pagsanjan 94, 157
Pajares, Francisco Marcos, OSA IX
Panay VI, XV, 1, 4, 5, 7, 31, 56, 59, 61, 63, 99, 127, 141
Pandora's box 12
Paracelsus 150
Paraclete 36, 46, 47
parousia 107, 125
Pascal 76
Pascual, Evangeline X
Pasig River 52, 157
Pegasus 25
people of God 21
Peru IX
Pharisaical 11
Pharisee 12, 39
Philippine art and literature 76

Philippine Collegian 7
Philippine National Artist for Literature 121
Philippine Priests' Forum 7
Philippines II, IX, X, XI, XIII, XIV, XV, XVI, 1, 2, 6, 34, 56, 59, 60, 64, 69, 79, 80, 85, 91, 101, 115, 122, 123, 124, 127, 128, 129, 131, 132, 133, 134, 145, 146, 147, 151, 153, 155, 156, 157
Philippine Studies 7, 141
Picasso 75
Pineda, R. V. 42
Plato 26, 52, 132
poetry II, XI, XIII, XIV, XV, XVI, 1, 3, 4, 6, 8, 18, 30, 47, 64, 72, 75, 78, 91, 100, 112, 114, 115, 116, 122, 123, 126, 132, 136, 138, 142, 145, 146, 150, 153
Polotan, Kerima X
Polpulan 58
Pope Francis XIII, XIV
Poulsen, Therese Cindy C. Garnado IX
Prague 23, 24
pre-Vatican II 1, 18, 20, 33
Prometheus 77
Propaganda Movement 79
Protestant XIV, XVII, 4, 8, 18, 19, 100, 115, 123, 153
Proust 76
Province of the Most Holy Name of Jesus of the Philippines IX
psychic experience 31

Q

Quezon City 1, 2, 3, 7, 8, 59, 60, 64, 68, 69, 70, 85, 91, 101, 107, 112, 115, 119, 127, 128, 137
Quiapo 104, 157

R

rebellious sonnets 16
religion and superstition VI, 59
religious poet II, XIII, XVII, 4, 5, 6, 9, 27, 29, 30, 102, 123, 125
Rembrandt 75
Republic Cultural Heritage Award for Literature 6
resurrection 28
Rishi Lakshman 59
Rizal 6, 76, 77, 79, 105, 144
Roces, Alejandro X
Rockefeller Fellowship XIV
Rodríguez Rodríguez, Father Isacio, OSA X
Rojo, Father Nicéforo, OSA XI
Roman Catholic XIII
Romualdez Marcos, Imelda 133, 155
Romulo, Carlos P. 64
Russia 69

S

Saénz de Santa María, Rafael X
Saint Augustine XI, 76, 83, 120, 137, 142, 150, 152, 154
Saint Cyprian 28, 29, 137
Saint Francis 2, 109, 110, 111, 138, 140, 141, 144
Saint Michael 74
San Agustín Church 2, 111, 122, 157
Sands and Coral XIV
San Juan de la Cruz 3
Santos, Felixberto 7
Santos, María Paz X
Sanzio 74
Sanzio, the Lord of Order, 74
Satan 73, 74
Schwartz, Delmore XIV
Scylla and Charybdis 76
Serna Ares, Jesús Gregorio X
Sicio Pingol, Father Rodolfo, OSA X
signs of the times 22
Silliman University XIV, 134
Sionil José, F. X, 145
Sister Candelaria de la Inmaculada, OSA X
Sister Lorenza Gequillana, OSA X
Sister Martha 23, 24
Sister Salome de la Inmaculada Concepción, OSA X
Sobrepeña, Reverend David A. 115
Society of Saint Paul X
Solidarity 7, 65, 128, 129, 144, 145
Sophocles 26
Southeast Asia Writer's Award 6
Spain X, XVII, 3, 74, 79
Spaniards 78, 155, 156
Spanish Basque IX
statue of David 24
Statue of Liberty 24
Stendhal 75
St. John-Perse 75
Stygian sty 74
Suárez García, Father Restituto X
sui generis XIII, 3, 4, 123
Sumakwel 56, 59, 60, 61, 62, 146
Supreme Being 5, 123
Szu Kung Tu 74

T

Tabuena, Romeo 81
Tagore 74
Tankiang, Paquito X
Tatad, Francisco S. X
Tate, Allen XIV
Templo Redublo, Nati X
Teresa de Ávila 3
the artist's genius 66
Theban 25
The City and the Thread of Light VII, 1, 2, 4, 5, 7, 100, 101, 102, 104, 111, 121, 127, 129
The Diliman Review 2, 131, 141, 144
The Golden Legend 150
The Golden Mean VI, 48
The Heart of Emptiness Is Black XV, 3, 56, 58, 59, 60, 62, 63, 150, 152
The Philwomanian 102
The Scare-Crow Christ VI, XV, 1, 2, 4, 5, 85, 88, 91, 95, 97, 127, 131, 141, 144, 146, 148
The Second Vatican Council 100
The Silliman University National Writers Workshop 134
the way of the flesh VI, 31
Third World 79
Thomas, Dylan XV, 14
Tiempo, Edilberto XIV, 129, 130, 134
Tiempo, Edith 134
Tinio, Rolando 146, 149
Tondo 104, 157
toro 157
Torres, Emmanuel 146
Tramble, Father Eugene, OSA XI
Tu Fu 74
twentieth-century mind 31
tyranny 77

U

United States II, XI, 30, 79, 137
University of Iowa XIV, 4
University of Santo Tomás XI
University of the Philippines IX, XIII, XIV, XVI, 1, 6, 56, 59, 60, 64, 69, 85, 91, 101, 115, 123, 131, 134, 147
U.P. Newsletter 42, 129
U.P. Press 141
U.P. Writers Summer Workshop 42
U.P. Writers Workshop 134
Urrutia Anda, Father Felix, OSA X

V

Valera, Amelia I. X
Van Gogh 71, 72
Vara, Father Moises, OSA X
Vatican Radio XIII
Vega Blanco, Father Tirso, OSA X
Vega, C.M. X
Vermeer 75
Viray, Manuel E. 146

W

Western Visayas 151, 156
White, Helen C. 4
White, Janet Frances II, XI

Writers & Their Milieu XIV, 130
Writer's Union of the Philippines Award 6

Y

Yabes, Dean Leopoldo Y. XVI, 40
Yeats, W.B. XV

Z

Zóbel, Fernando 81

www.ingramcontent.com/pod-product-compliance
Lightning Source LLC
LaVergne TN
LVHW040115080426
835507LV00039B/376